THE P...

FOUNDER EDI...

PR...

Betty R...

FLAVIUS PHILOSTRAT... origin, his family reputed... Athens before going to Rome, ... 'salon' of Julia Domna, wife of the emperor Septimus Severus. At the request of the empress he wrote his famous account of Apollonius of Tyana. He was also the author of other works, the best known being his *Lives of the Sophists*, a series of anecdotal biographies of the leaders of the so-called Second Sophistic. Philostratus died between A.D. 244 and 249.

CHRISTOPHER P. JONES was born at Chislehurst, Kent, in 1940, and educated at Rugby School and Balliol College, Oxford. Since receiving his Ph.D. at Harvard University in 1965 he has taught at the University of Toronto, where he is an Associate Professor of Classics. His main interest is in the social and economic history of the high Roman Empire. He has published on this and other subjects in a variety of learned journals, and is now writing a book on *Plutarch and Rome*.

G. W. BOWERSOCK was born in Providence, Rhode Island, U.S.A., in 1936, and educated at Harvard and (as a Rhodes Scholar) at Balliol College, Oxford. After teaching ancient history at Oxford he returned to Harvard, where he is now Professor of Greek and Latin. He has written two books: *Augustus and the Greek World* and *Greek Sophists in the Roman Empire*. He is now writing a history of the Roman province of Arabia.

PHILOSTRATUS

LIFE OF APOLLONIUS

TRANSLATED BY
C. P. JONES
EDITED, ABRIDGED
AND INTRODUCED BY
G. W. BOWERSOCK

PENGUIN BOOKS

Penguin Books Ltd, Harmondsworth, Middlesex, England
Penguin Books Inc., 7110 Ambassador Road, Baltimore, Maryland 21207, U.S.A.
Penguin Books Australia Ltd, Ringwood, Victoria, Australia

—

This edition first published 1970

—

Copyright © C. P. Jones, 1970
Introduction and notes copyright © G. W. Bowersock, 1970

—

Made and printed in Great Britain
by Richard Clay (The Chaucer Press) Ltd,
Bungay, Suffolk
Set in Monotype Bembo

CONTENTS

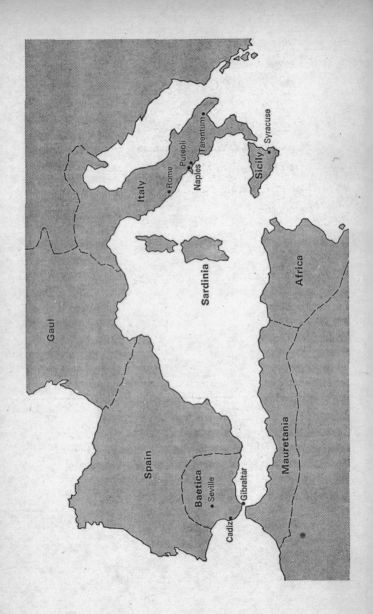

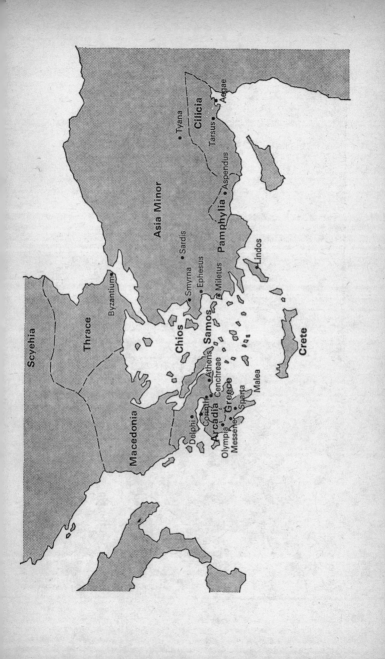

Scythia

Thrace

Macedonia

Byzantium

Asia Minor

Tyana

Cilicia

Aegae

Tarsus

Pamphylia

Aspendus

Sardis

Smyrna

Ephesus

Miletus

Lindos

Chios

Samos

Athens

Cenchreae

Corinth

Delphi

Arcadia

Olympia

Greece

Messene

Sparta

Malea

Crete

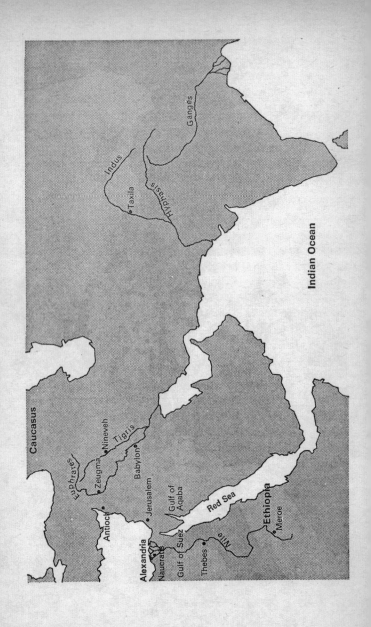

INTRODUCTION

NOT a scrap of secure contemporary evidence survives to illuminate the career of Apollonius, the wise man of Tyana. It is extraordinary that this minor mystic, from a remote city in Cappadocia, should have acquired long after his death no less a reputation than that of an anti-Christ. Apollonius raised the dead, healed the sick, and ascended bodily into heaven: so, at least, his biographer Philostratus affirms. Some labelled him a philosopher, some a magician or wizard. His home-made sandals, his uncut hair, his simple clothing, his abstention from the sacrifice of living things, proclaimed him a follower of the ancient sage, Pythagoras. Apollonius was a neo-Pythagorean, one of life's committed non-conformists whose pursuit of truth and sincerity brought him into conflict with the established government of his time. Philostratus saw in this eccentric worker of miracles a magnificent subject for romantic and legendary biography. For Philostratus Apollonius was not an anti-Christ, but in his biography he provided the stories which made him one.

Philostratus must have completed the biography in the vicinity of the year A.D. 220. He undertook the work, as he himself declares, at the request of the Syrian empress Julia Domna, wife of Septimius Severus; and yet Philostratus did not dedicate the finished biography to her. Scholars have inferred from this omission that Julia was no longer alive. As she died in A.D. 217, the biography of Apollonius was completed in all probability after that year.

Julia Domna was a remarkable woman. She was stylish in her coiffure, dedicated to culture, and politically ambitious.

When, toward the end of the second century, she found her ambitions thwarted by Severus's powerful prefect of the praetorian guard, Fulvius Plautianus, she concentrated her energies upon the formation of a circle of philosophers and literary men. Modern students of the age of Septimius Severus have tended to overrate the influence of Julia's salon and carelessly to lodge in it most of the intellectual luminaries of the day. Yet to deny that Julia's friends were persons of importance is not to deny the importance of the circle. Philostratus was by his own admission a member of it, and the biography of Apollonius came into being because of it. A descendant of one of the sage's closest followers had, we are told, brought to the empress's attention certain memoirs from the pen of his kinsman, and Julia instructed Philostratus to prepare a biography on the basis of those long neglected documents.

It may be that the memoirs, ascribed to a certain Damis of Nineveh, never existed: Philostratus, a good rhetorician and sophist from a family of sophists, might well have invoked a non-existent source so as to give an air of authority to his narrative. Many readers of his work have been firm in branding Damis a fiction on the basis of historical improbabilities that ill become an eyewitness account.[1] However that may be, the patronage of Julia is not in doubt. Her circle evidently had some interest in Apollonius, but reliable information about him was scarce.

Apollonius was apparently born in the early years of the Christian era and – if Philostratus can be trusted – he perished at an advanced age during the short reign of Nerva, emperor from A.D. 96 to 98. Certain of his letters survived, for the emperor Hadrian had a collection of them. Philostratus also had access to letters of Apollonius, some of which overlap

1. The problem of Damis is discussed in greater detail below, pp. 17–19.

with a collection still extant. However, some (though certainly not all) of the letters in Philostratus's work and in the separate collection are ancient forgeries, therefore treacherous documents from which to draw historical conclusions. Moreover, it seems that certain other writings of Apollonius survived in addition to various letters. There were, for instance, a treatise on sacrifices and a biography of Pythagoras.

Further pre-Philostratean evidence for Apollonius lay in the four books devoted to the sage by one Moeragenes. These books no longer exist, and Philostratus claims largely to have ignored them because they were untrustworthy. The Christian writer, Origen, a younger contemporary of Philostratus, also refers to Moeragenes's work on Apollonius; and from his comment it appears that the account was hostile, perhaps incorporating the views of Apollonius's greatest enemy, the long-bearded philosopher Euphrates. Philostratus makes reference to another source that was available to him, namely an account of what Apollonius did in the Cilician city of Aegae. This source and its author, a Maximus of Aegae, have been called into question by modern scholars; but the case is different from that of Damis. Philostratus guarantees the reality of Maximus when he indicates his position in the Roman civil service. Maximus was in charge of the emperor's Greek correspondence (*ab epistulis graecis*). That post cannot have had a fictitious incumbent.

Apart from the letters, the sources available to Philostratus are lost to us. For the long period from Apollonius's death to Philostratus's biography, there is scarcely a reference to the man who was destined for such notoriety. Lucian, satirist and essayist of second-century Hellenism, is the only writer before Philostratus to refer explicitly to Apollonius; and what he has to say is not complimentary. He alludes to the paederasty and nonsense of Apollonius's adherents. Lucian's passing reference reflects a hostile tradition of which Moeragenes's four books doubtless formed a more substantial example. One could easily imagine what a rhetorically perfected denunciation of Apollonius would have looked like. There would have been much on sexual licence and corruption, elaborate illustrations of the babblings of a demonically possessed wizard, and (as can be seen from the charges which Philostratus makes Apollonius answer) chilling descriptions of dining on the flesh of infants. There is no sign that hagiography of the Philostratean kind was in vogue before the circle of Julia Domna turned its attention to Apollonius. Philostratus significantly emphasizes the incredible chastity of the sage, his deep philosophical wisdom, and his simple eating.

It will not have been an accident that the figure of Apollonius suddenly became conspicuous in Roman history not long before Julia Domna's death. In the year 215 her son, the emperor Caracalla, as he marched with his entourage through Cappadocia, paused at Tyana to honour the memory of Apollonius, and ordered a shrine to be built. His mother Julia was with him at the time. The event was recorded by a distinguished contemporary of Philostratus, the historian Cassius Dio. And it is not only in his account of Caracalla in the East that Dio mentions Apollonius: his narrative of the murder of Domitian includes a miraculous vision of Apollonius at Ephesus, a vision reported in similar terms by Philostratus himself. Apollonius beheld the scene of Domitian's murder while it was actually happening, despite the vast distance that lay between the emperor at Rome and the sage at Ephesus.

Severus Alexander, who came to the throne in A.D. 222, following upon the extravagant Heliogabalus, ruled Rome in the later years of both Philostratus and Cassius Dio. It is therefore of interest to note that Alexander is alleged by the author (or authors) of the so-called *Augustan History* to have kept in his private shrine the images of four men: Abraham, Orpheus, Christ and Apollonius. This testimony, credible to a degree, is nevertheless suspect; the conjunction of Apollonius and Christ belongs to another age. The juxtaposition of these two personalities is a part of the later struggle of paganism and Christianity, and one may legitimately assume that the text which preserves that item about Severus Alexander and his shrine simply mirrors the preoccupations of its own time. The *Augustan History* is a notoriously unreliable work, in which fiction proliferates. The same work declares, for example, that the emperor Aurelian spared the city of Tyana as the result of an epiphany of the long dead Apollonius. There is no truth in this.

The parallelism of Apollonius and Christ seems first to have been developed during the Diocletianic persecution of the Christians. A certain Hierocles, who governed the province of Bithynia at that time, composed an anti-Christian tract, entitled *The Lover of Truth*, in which Philostratus's eulogistic biography was plundered for proof that Apollonius of Tyana was Christ's equal. Hierocles's tract has not survived, but we are fortunate to possess an elaborate reply to it by Eusebius of Caesarea, who records the arguments and sometimes the words of Hierocles. It is evident that the principal ground of contention was the working of miracles. Hierocles spoke rudely of Peter and Paul in comparison with what he considered the unimpeachable sources for Apollonius; he made it a charge that Christians declared their Saviour a god on the strength of a few paltry miracles, whereas Apollonius, who accomplished more and greater, was reckoned only a man but a man welcome to the gods.

It is clear that by the end of the fourth century Apollonius of Tyana had become a figure of importance in the great struggle of the pagans against the Christians. Philostratus's biography was translated into Latin, and the translation itself subsequently revised. The notices concerning Apollonius in the *Augustan History* are but another manifestation of the significance of Apollonius in the later age, if the composition of that work be assigned (as it should) to the last decade of the fourth century. St Augustine was obliged to declare the absurdity of ranking the sage of Tyana above Jesus Christ; but, in the hierarchy of pagan worthies, he ranked Apollonius above Zeus himself. Byzantine Christianity continued this obsession with him and even managed eventually to accommodate him in the figurative decoration of churches. He ultimately passed into Arabic legend as Balinas, master of talismans.

In all probability the biography of Apollonius by Philostratus was the cause and fundamental text of the great posthumous revival. Hierocles depended upon Philostratus's work and the memoirs it claimed to follow; the late fourth century exhibits translations and revisions of translations. Before Philostratus the traces of Apollonius are very slight indeed. It may be more accurate to credit the empress Julia Domna and her circle, for Philostratus must mirror their enthusiasms. But he obviously attacked his subject with a relish of his own. The *Life of Apollonius* is a long and elaborate work to which Philostratus devoted himself even when Julia was dead.

Philostratus belonged to a literary family from the island of Lemnos. The precise details of his family are by no means as clear as scholars would wish, but there can be little doubt that both antecedents and descendants were fashionable men of letters, rhetors, or rather (to use the proper term) sophists. They bore the Roman family name of Flavius and were a part of the conspicuous literary renaissance in the Greek world under Roman rule, a renaissance of which Philostratus was himself a chronicler. He named it the 'Second Sophistic' when he wrote the biographies of its chief representatives in his *Lives of the Sophists*. His subjects were polished and cultivated orators who enjoyed social eminence and political power in the second and early third centuries. They were to be distinguished from the sophists of the fifth and fourth century B.C., men like Gorgias and Isocrates: hence the term Second Sophistic. The heroes of Philostratus were men like Polemo of Laodicea and the fabulously rich Herodes Atticus of Athens. Several of the sophists of whom Philostratus wrote in his *Lives* were his own teachers.

The biography of Apollonius was composed before the *Lives of the Sophists*, for the latter work alludes to the former. In writing about Apollonius, Philostratus was himself practising the sophistic arts; this was at a time before he stood back to survey the whole movement to which he was heir. The *Life of Apollonius* is a characteristic product of its time (like the circle of Julia itself). It is an elaborate and romantic novel, picaresque, with a historical context, and generously equipped with exotica. Its descriptions of the wonders of India and Ethiopia link it with the abundant contemporary literature of travel (real and imaginary), of which Lucian's *True History* is a gloriously irreverent parody. The unfolding of a narrative in the course of such geographical excursuses indicates the close affinity of Philostratus's book with the contemporary romantic novel, although that (to be sure) was stronger in the erotic line. The apologetic character of the biography – one thinks above all of the vast speech of Apollonius to Domitian near the end – suggests literary connexions with the so-called Acts of the Pagan Martyrs. These were pagan equivalents of saints' lives, and they contained defiant speeches of courageous pagans against established authority. The Acts of the Pagan Martyrs form a part of the developing tradition of biography under the Roman Empire, a tradition given special impetus by Suetonius and Plutarch.

Philostratus as the author of the life of Apollonius was, therefore, a literary man of his age. He wrote as a sophist when he composed Apollonius's speech to Domitian. It is a rhetorical showpiece, dazzling and unhistorical; Philostratus knew his craft. He was amply qualified to write a history of the Second Sophistic later in life and thereby to become a kind of historian. But it is significant that the later work was also accomplished in the biographical form. Yet between the *Lives of the Sophists* and the *Life of Apollonius* there is a huge gulf. The historical details which Philostratus provides about the sophists are not generally open to question, whereas in the case of Apollonius the separation of fact from fiction, so consummate was Philostratus's art, is a task of frustrating delicacy. Ancient writers, pagan and Christian alike, were disinclined to make the effort; they were content to argue from Philostratus's evidence as given. Modern scholars have, however, probed the historical accuracy of the *Life of Apollonius* over and over again. There is still no agreement.

Somehow the historian must sort out what is pure invention (like the speech to Domitian), what is legend, and what is historical fact. This is, of course, a standard problem in assessing any historical novel; but rarely does a novel supply, where information is scarce, attractive pieces of historical evidence that are nowhere else to be found. The easiest way out of the problem of the historical trustworthiness of Philostratus's biography is naturally to refuse to credit anything unless it is already otherwise attested. This melancholy attitude saves thought but elicits justified censure. After all, some of the items in the biography are demonstrably true. Vardanes, the king in Babylon, is placed in a chronological context (the reign of Claudius) that coincides with other evidence; Domitian's measure against castration and his vine edict, both mentioned at the end of Book Six, are indisputably historical. But then, is the role of Apollonius in the response to the vine edict also historical? The astute reader of Philostratus's work will have, however uncomfortably, to hover at all times between total belief and total disbelief. Each item has to be tested on its own merits.

There is, however, one basic issue which requires a decision: the notebooks of Damis. If this source, upon which Philostratus claims to rely so heavily, is genuine, then belief in historical details that are otherwise unattested will be considerably facilitated. Damis, we are told, was a contemporary witness. In recent times most scholars, unlike the authors of antiquity, have rejected Damis and his notebooks as complete fabrications of Philostratus, who would have introduced them solely to give an air of weight and authority to his own free invention. The citation of Damis gives the biography a scholarly veneer. The rejection of Damis cannot, of course, entail the rejection of other sources cited by Philostratus: the work of Moeragenes, for example, is independently attested by Origen, who had read it. Real and imaginary sources side by side: that is not inconceivable. The *Augustan History* shows the same symbiosis. Damis is suspect for the very reason that so much is ascribed to him.

If the Philostratean Damis can be convicted of gross historical inaccuracy about what is allegedly his own time, then it is quite right to condemn him as a credible source. Three cases may be adduced here. The first concerns the Cynic philosopher Demetrius, who (as Tacitus and others reveal) flourished in the time of Nero. Philostratus's account of Demetrius in Books Four and Five, an account expressly connected with the testimony of Damis, cannot be reconciled with the facts of Roman history. According to Philostratus, Demetrius spoke out against the construction of Nero's new gymnasium and as a result incurred the wrath of the prefect of the praetorian guard, Tigellinus, who expelled him from Rome. Now we happen to know that the building of the gymnasium belongs to the years A.D. 60–62: at that time Tigellinus, who later became notorious, was not yet prefect. Furthermore, in Philostratus's own narrative, when Apollonius comes to Rome in the year A.D. 66 (a date guaranteed by references to the consul Telesinus, a real person known to have been consul in 66), Demetrius is then in Rome. Back so soon from an exile which is dated by a chronological impossibility? In the next year Apollonius finds Demetrius in Athens, in exile and, we are told, precisely because of that speech of at least five years earlier against the gymnasium.

The only believable part of this whole collection of anecdotes is that Demetrius was in exile in Greece after 66. The rest is hopelessly confused. It takes a mighty faith (some scholars have it) to think that an eyewitness, such as Damis, could have made chronological blunders of the most elementary kind. Whoever compounded the stories of Apollonius and Demetrius (and Philostratus seems the obvious candidate) had heard of the gymnasium, of Telesinus, of Demetrius's exile; but he had no very exact knowledge of the history of Nero's reign.

A second illustration of the inaccuracy of Philostratus and Damis: Vindex's revolt against Nero in March 68. In Book Five Apollonius is credited with stirring up support for the revolt of Julius Vindex in Gaul. This took place, we are told, when Nero was on his artistic tour in Greece. The simultaneity is false, for Nero was back in Italy when Vindex took up arms. Would an eyewitness make so elementary a slip?

A third illustration: In Book Seven Domitian is said to have exiled the future emperor Nerva to the town of Tarentum. Now it is known that Domitian wanted to kill him but desisted because he was told that Nerva, a man of advanced age, would die within a few days. There is no indication that he was exiled to Tarentum; but it was precisely to Tarentum that Nerva himself, as emperor, exiled a conspirator, a certain Calpurnius Crassus. Patently some later writer (why not Philostratus?) has muddled his evidence about Nerva and an exile at Tarentum.

These items should suffice to show the kinds of reason for which the Damis source and the historical reliability of

Philostratus's novel have been discredited. It is clear, however, that where there is error in the narrative there is also truth. Tigellinus *was* a Neronian prefect and Telesinus a Neronian consul; Domitian *did* want to get rid of Nerva. The separation of fact from fiction in the *Life of Apollonius* has to be a distinct and careful operation in every case. The meeting of Vespasian, Apollonius, Dio Chrysostom and the philosopher Euphrates in Egypt contains much that is routine sophistic discourse on the ideal ruler (a beloved theme). But even if Philostratus be thought to have composed the speeches of the four men out of his own head, must one also assume that he brought them together in his work so as to effect the confrontation? The answer ought probably to be affirmative, and yet chronologically the presence of the four in Egypt is by no means impossible.

It might have been easier to believe in the existence of Damis's memoirs if there were any other trace of them at all. There is not. But it should be recalled that Philostratus's contemporary, the historian Cassius Dio, gives an account of Apollonius's vision of the murder of Domitian in language that is at several points extraordinarily close to that of Philostratus (relying on Damis). Dio's story contains the names of the men who plotted and acted against the emperor; Philostratus omits all but one of them, although he too probably knew them since the information was not obscure. The consonance of Dio and Philostratus here cannot be taken with certainty as more than another indication of the new interest in Apollonius in their day. It is likely that Dio had actually seen Philostratus's text. There remains, to be sure, the inevitable possibility of a common source, not – as Damis's papers purport to be – contemporary with the event; but at this point speculation loses its contact with substantive evidence.

★

Philostratus's *Life of Apollonius* has been infrequently translated into English. In 1680 Charles Blount published a version of the first two books with a declaration that he had actually translated the whole work. But he never released the rest because of an outcry that alerted him to the dangers of doing so. It would appear that publication in the vernacular was considered a threat to the Christian religion.

The first complete translation was published in 1809 by the Rev. Edward Berwick. His reason for making the translation proves that the old arguments about Apollonius and Christ were still not dead. The Rev. Berwick's own words deserve quotation:

I have only now to add, that had any English translation of the work existed, I should not have undertaken the present one, which is submitted with the greatest deference to the public, in the hopes that it will fully serve to set in its true light the character of Apollonius and to wipe away an uncandid insinuation of Mr Gibbon, who seems glad (as he does on every occasion) to fix a stigma on the Divine Author of our religion: an insinuation which I believe he never would have made, had any translation of the work been extant in his own language, to which the reader might have had an easy access. The insinuation I allude to, is couched in a note to the first volume of his Roman History, in which he wishes to confound the character of our blessed Saviour, with that of an impostor and a magician, though the dissimilarity, in every point of view, is so great between the two persons, that one is surprised how the liberal candour of a gentleman and a scholar, could adopt it, and give it to a discerning public. In fine, if I should succeed in removing this unfair and unfounded imputation, I will think myself well repaid for the time and trouble expended in this work.

What Edward Gibbon had said was this: 'Apollonius of Tyana was born about the same time as Jesus Christ. His life (that of the former) is related in so fabulous a manner by his fanatic disciples, that we are at a loss to discover whether he was a sage, or an impostor.' The Rev. Berwick in a note describes Gibbon's comment as 'a sneer, which is but an expression of ludicrous scorn'.

It was not too many years later, in 1832, that a German theologian, Ferdinand Christian Baur, presented a famous study of Apollonius and Christ, in which he contended that Philostratus himself had written the biography as an instrument of anti-Christian propaganda. No reputable scholar would hold this opinion any more, but it died slowly.

After the pious exertions of the Rev. Berwick, Philostratus's work was not translated again into English until the early twentieth century. The Loeb translation, by F. C. Conybeare, and the Oxford translation, by J. S. Phillimore, both appeared, curiously, in the same year, 1912. The new English version by C. P. Jones is, therefore, only the fourth (if we exclude Blount's); it sets an unprecedentedly high standard of accuracy, felicity and clarity in the rendering of Philostratus's difficult Greek.

As the first translations of the *Life of Apollonius* amply testify, this work has been, in the modern world no less than in the ancient, closely bound up with the history and defence of Christianity. Yet it has had its influence in secular literature. Robert Burton, in the *Anatomy of Melancholy* (1621), rendered the story of Apollonius and the lady-vampire at Corinth in what is nearly a direct translation of Philostratus. Burton's words inspired John Keats in 1819 to compose his poem entitled *Lamia*. For *lamia* is a word used in Philostratus's Greek to denominate the vampire, and the term had been taken over by Burton in his version of the story. It is odd that with Berwick's translation available to him Keats came to Apollonius only through the mediation of Burton. However that may be, it is marvellous to hear the echoes of Philostratus in the romantic pentameters of an age far removed and to meet Apollonius again:

So in they hurried all, 'mazed, curious and keen,
Save one, who looked thereon with eye severe,
And with calm-planted steps walked in austere;
'Twas Apollonius: something too he laughed,
As though some knotty problem, that had daft
His patient thought, had now begun to thaw,
And solve and melt – 'twas just as he foresaw.

Cambridge, Massachusetts   G. W. BOWERSOCK

ROMAN EMPERORS

in whose reigns Apollonius lived

AUGUSTUS	27 B.C.–A.D. 14
TIBERIUS	14–37
GAIUS (CALIGULA)	37–41
CLAUDIUS	41–54
NERO	54–68
GALBA	68–69
OTHO	69
VITELLIUS	69
VESPASIAN	69–79
TITUS	79–81
DOMITIAN	81–96
NERVA	96–98

BIBLIOGRAPHY

*This is a brief, selective list
for readers interested in investigating
the scholarly literature on Philostratus's*
Life of Apollonius

F. CHR. BAUR, *Apollonius von Tyana und Christus*, 1832.

K. I. MILLER, 'Zur Frage nach der Persönlichkeit des Apollonius von Tyana', *Philologus* 51, 1892, 581 ff.
'Die Damispapiere in Philostratos' Apollonius-biographie', *Philologus* 66, 1907, 511 ff.

E. MEYER, 'Apollonios von Tyana und die Biographie des Philostratos', *Hermes* 52, 1917, 371 ff.

J. MESK, 'Die Damisquelle des Philostratus in der Biographie des Apollonius von Tyana', *Wiener Studien* 61, 1919, 121 ff.

J. HEMPEL, *Untersuchungen zur Überlieferung von Apollonius von Tyana*, Beiträge z. Religionswissenschaft 4, 1920.

TH. HOPFNER, 'Apollonius von Tyana und Philostratus', *Seminar Kondakov* 4, 1931, 135 ff.

B. A. VAN GRONINGEN, 'Apollonius de Tyane', *Bulletin de la faculté des lettres de Strasbourg* 30, 1951–2, 107 ff.

F. GROSSO, 'La vita di Apollonio di Tiana come fonte storica', *Acme* 7, 1954, 333 ff.

NOTE ON THE TEXT

Philostratus's original biography is lengthy. It has been abridged in this translation by the omission of certain unimportant digressions and specimens of overblown rhetoric. The result, it is hoped, will be somewhat more readable. However, many of the digressions and speeches still remain in this version: to remove them in bulk would be to destroy the character of the work.

The translation has been made from the Teubner text of C. L. Kayser.

BOOK I

1. According to his followers, Pythagoras of Samos was not really an Ionian, but had once been Euphorbus in the Trojan war. Euphorbus died, as the poems of Homer relate,[1] but after his death he came to life again. He shunned clothing made from animal-skins, and abstained from all food or sacrifices of living creatures, since he never defiled altars with blood; instead he offered honey-cakes, frankincense and hymns to the gods. He knew that such things were more welcome to them than sacrifices of many animals and the knife laid on the sacred basket, for he had conversed with the gods and learnt what makes them angry or pleased with mankind. It was from such conversations that he explained their nature; others, he said, merely made inferences about the divine and had conflicting views about it, whereas he had been visited by Apollo appearing without disguise and also, though this time disguised, by Athena, the Muses, and other gods, whose shapes and names were quite unknown to men.

All Pythagoras's revelations his disciples considered law, and they honoured him as a messenger from Zeus. Hence they practised silence on celestial subjects: they had heard many sacred secrets which they could hardly have kept had they not learnt that even silence is a form of discourse. They say that Empedocles of Acragas followed the same school of wisdom: for his verses, 'Farewell, I am an immortal god to you and no longer a mortal' and 'Once I was both girl and boy' and the ox which he is said to have made out of pastry and sacrificed at Olympia are perhaps signs that he approved of Pythagoras's

1. cf. *Iliad* XVII. 43–60.

doctrines. Many more things are told about those who practise Pythagoras's form of wisdom, but it is not my business to go into them here, being eager to proceed with the account that I have set myself to give.

2. The practices of Apollonius were very like this, and he studied wisdom in a more inspired way than Pythagoras; he also despised tyrannies. Yet, although he lived in times which were neither ancient nor modern, people do not know him for the genuine wisdom which he practised as a philosopher and an honourable man. Instead some single out only one or two of his virtues; others, because of his association with Babylonian magicians, Indian Brahmans, and the Naked Philosophers of Egypt, think him a magician and misrepresent him as an intruder into philosophy. This is a misjudgement. Empedocles, Pythagoras himself and Democritus associated with magicians and said many inspired things without being seduced by the art. Plato too went to Egypt, where he picked up much from the local prophets and priests, and mixed it into his own doctrines like a painter adding colour to a sketch, and yet he was never thought a magician, even though he was resented for his wisdom more than any man.

Nor should Apollonius's frequent presentiments and prophecies give him a reputation for practising that kind of wisdom, or else Socrates will get the same reputation because of the foreknowledge he received from his guardian spirit, and Anaxagoras because of his predictions. It is common knowledge that once at Olympia there had been no rain at all, and Anaxagoras came into the stadium wearing a sheepskin, thus prophesying rain; and when he predicted that a certain house would collapse it did and he was proved right. Similarly, when he proclaimed that the day would turn into night and that stones would fall out of the sky at Aegospotami, his words came true. Yet people ascribe all this to Anaxagoras's wisdom, while denying that Apollonius's foreknowledge came from the same source, as if it was magic by which he did such things.

I have therefore decided to do something about this widespread misconception and give an accurate account of Apollonius, observing the chronology of his words and acts and the special character of the wisdom that brought him close to being thought possessed and inspired. I have gathered my materials partly from the many cities that were devoted to him, partly from the shrines which he set right when their rules had fallen into neglect, partly from what others have said about him and partly from his own letters.[2] For he corresponded with kings, sophists, philosophers, Eleans, Delphians, Indians, Egyptians. He wrote about the gods, about customs, morals and laws; and when wrong was done, he tried to put it right.

3. But my more detailed information I have gathered from a quite cultivated man called Damis who once lived in ancient Nineveh. This man became a disciple of Apollonius and has left an account of his master's journeys, on which he claims to have accompanied him, and also an account of his sayings, speeches and predictions. The notebooks containing the memoirs of Damis were unknown until a member of his family brought them to the attention of the empress Julia.[3] Since I was a member of her salon (for she admired and encouraged every branch of rhetoric), she set me to transcribe these discourses of Damis. I was to pay particular attention to

2. A collection of letters of Apollonius survives from antiquity (see the Introduction, pp. 10–11 above).

3. The empress is Julia Domna, the Syrian wife of Septimius Severus, who ruled A.D. 193–211. One presumes that Julia is dead at the time Philostratus is writing: the life of Apollonius is not dedicated to her. She died in A.D. 217.

their style, for the man from Nineveh had a clear one, but rather artless. I have also read the book of Maximus of Aegae, which contains all that Apollonius did there, and the will written by Apollonius himself, which gives an idea of how inspired he was in his philosophy. But it is best to ignore the four books which Moeragenes composed about Apollonius, because of the great ignorance of their subject that they display. So much for the way I gathered my material from different sources and the care I took to assemble it.[4] I hope that my work will bring credit to the man who is its concern and profit to those with some interest in learning: for they really might learn things of which at present they have no idea.

4. Apollonius came from Tyana, a Greek city in the country of Cappadocia. His father had the same name as himself, and the family was an old one that went back to the founders of the city. Its wealth was exceptional there, even though it is a rich country. When his mother was still carrying him, she had a vision of an Egyptian spirit, Proteus, whom Homer describes changing into different shapes.[5] She was not frightened at all, but asked him who her child would be. He replied: 'Me.' 'Who are you?' she asked, and he said, 'Proteus, the Egyptian god.' Now if my readers have read the poets there is no point in my describing how wise Proteus was, how clever and various and elusive, and how he seemed to have all knowledge and foreknowledge. But the reader must bear Proteus in mind, especially when the course of my story shows that Apollonius had greater foreknowledge than he had, and proved himself the master of many difficult and baffling situations just when he seemed to be trapped.

4. On Maximus and Moeragenes, see the Introduction, pp. 11-12 above.

5. cf. *Odyssey* IV. 417-18.

5. Apollonius is said to have been born in a meadow, near which an elaborate temple now stands in his honour. The way he was born is worth knowing. His mother was near her time when she was told in a dream to go to a meadow and gather flowers. When she got there her servant girls wandered over the meadow with their minds on the flowers, while she lay down in the grass and fell asleep. As she slept, some swans that fed there formed a circle around her, and raising their wings in the way they do made a sudden noise, for there was a slight breeze in the meadow. The sound made her jump up and give birth, any excitement being enough to cause birth even before the due time. The local people also say that the moment Apollonius was born a bolt of lightning which seemed just about to strike the earth hung poised in the air and then disappeared upwards; no doubt the gods were giving a revelation – an omen of his brilliance, his exaltation above earthly things, his closeness to heaven, and all his other qualities.

6. They say there is a well near Tyana called the well of Asbama, sacred to Zeus the Guardian of Oaths. A spring of cold water rises there which bubbles like a cauldron on the fire. Those who keep their word find the water pleasant and safe, but when perjurers drink it their punishment is at hand, for in fact it attacks their eyes, their hands and their feet; and they themselves catch dropsy or consumption. Unable even to leave the place, they are caught there, groaning by the fountain and confessing their perjuries. So the local people say that Apollonius was the son of Zeus, but he always refers to himself as the son of Apollonius.

7. When he reached the age for school, he showed a good memory and power of application; his Greek was of the Attic kind and his accent unaffected by the region. His beauty was

so conspicuous that he drew looks from every side. When he reached fourteen his father took him to Tarsus to learn from Euthydemus of Phoenicia. This man was a good rhetor as well as Apollonius's teacher, and Apollonius became devoted to him, though finding Tarsus corrupt in its ways and inimical to philosophy.[6] The people there are exceptionally given to luxury, all of them frivolous and insulting, and more devoted to fine linen clothing than the Athenians are to wisdom. There is a river flowing through their city, the Cydnus, beside which they sit like water-fowl, and that is why Apollonius says to them in a letter, 'Stop getting drunk on water.'

So with his father's permission he found a new teacher in Aegae nearby, where there was peace that encouraged a love of wisdom, and interests more suitable for young men: there is also a shrine of Asclepius, where Asclepius himself appears to men. There he had, as fellow-pupils, followers of Plato, Chrysippus and the Colonnade,[7] and he also heard the doctrines of Epicurus, not thinking even these unworthy of his attention: but those of Pythagoras he grasped by some mysterious intelligence.

His teacher in the doctrines of Pythagoras was not a very respectable man or one who put his philosophy into practice: he was too fond of food and sex and modelled himself on Epicurus. This man, Euxenus from Heracleia on the Pontus, understood the beliefs of Pythagoras as birds understand what they learn from men. 'Good day' and 'all the best' and 'good-bye' and so on are wishes that birds express without knowing what they mean or feeling any goodwill for us, but simply because they have been trained. But Apollonius was

6. This picture of Tarsus is supported by Strabo's account, pp. 672–4.

7. The Colonnade alludes to the Peripatetic school of philosophy, associated with Aristotle and Theophrastus. The colonnade in which the philosophers discoursed is called *peripatos* in Greek.

like those young eagles which, before their wings are fully developed, fly beside their parents as they learn the art of flight from them; when they are able to soar they rise higher than their parents, especially if they see that they are gluttons that keep near the ground to gorge themselves. Similarly Apollonius in his boyhood listened to Euxenus and was led by him along the path of reason: but when he reached fifteen he aspired to the life of a Pythagorean, to which some higher power gave him wings to climb.

He continued, however, to be a friend of Euxenus, and persuaded his father to give him a suburban estate with pleasant gardens and fountains in it. 'You live your own way,' he said, 'and I will live Pythagoras's way.' [8.] Euxenus thought he was undertaking an ambitious scheme, and asked him how he would begin. 'As doctors do,' he replied; 'they too purge their patients' stomachs and either prevent them from falling ill, or else cure them.' And after saying this he avoided the meat of animals as something impure that dulled the intelligence, and ate fruit and vegetables, saying that everything was pure which the earth produced of its own accord. Wine, he said, was a pure drink, since it came from a plant that had done such good to men, but it disturbed the balance of the mind by darkening the ether in the soul. After purging his stomach in this way he took to going barefoot (that was 'dressing' to him) and wore clothes of linen, refusing those that were made from animals. He also grew his hair long, and lived in the sanctuary. The inmates of it went in awe of him, and Asclepius told the priests that he was glad to cure the sick before the eyes of Apollonius. Thus people came to Aegae to satisfy their curiosity both from Cilicia and from the neighbouring regions; and the Cilician saying, 'Where are you off to? To see the young boy?' was first applied to Apollonius and acquired the status of a proverb.

9. As I am describing the life of a man whom even the gods thought highly of, it would not be right to pass over his actions in the shrine. A youth had come from Assyria to visit Asclepius, but indulged himself even on his sickbed; drinking was his whole life, or rather his death, for in fact he had dropsy and because of his love of wine was failing to dry up his condition. For this reason Asclepius did not help him or even visit him in his dreams. But when the youth reproached him for this he appeared to him and said, 'If you talk with Apollonius, you will be cured.' So he approached Apollonius and said, 'Asclepius has told me to converse with you: what can your wisdom do for me?'

'Something very valuable in your present condition,' was the reply, 'for I suppose you want a cure?'

'Indeed I do,' he said; 'a cure is what Asclepius has promised but not given me.'

'Don't blaspheme,' Apollonius said; 'he gives a cure to those who want it, but in your self-indulgence you are doing the opposite of what your disease requires. You are burdening your intestines with rich food when they are soft and bloated, and pouring water on mud.' These commandments were clearer, I think, than the wisdom of Heracleitus, who declared, when afflicted by the same disease, that he needed something to bring drought after a flood – a remark not at all comprehensible and clear, while Apollonius restored the youth to health by expressing himself wisely and simply.

10. Once he saw streams of blood on the altar and the victims laid out on it; Egyptian oxen and large pigs had been sacrificed, and men were flaying more and slaughtering others. Two gold vessels had been dedicated inset with marvellous stones, the most precious in India. Apollonius approached the priest, and said, 'What is all this? I see someone is giving the god expensive gifts.'

'You will be even more amazed,' said the other, 'to hear that he is making this expensive sacrifice without having been a suppliant here, or passing as much time here as the others, or being cured by the god, or obtaining what he came to ask for (I think he arrived yesterday). He says he will offer more sacrifices and more dedications if Asclepius listens to him. He is extremely rich, for he possesses a larger fortune in Cilicia than all the other Cilicians have between them, and he is begging the god to restore him the sight of one of his eyes.'

Apollonius fixed his glance on the ground, a habit he had in old age too, and asked, 'What is his name?' When he was told, he said, 'It seems to me, sire, that we should not admit this man to the shrine. He is somebody unclean, who met his affliction in shameful circumstances. For extravagant sacrifices offered when a man has not yet obtained anything from the god are not sacrifices, but excuses offered for shocking and wicked deeds.'

Apollonius said no more, but Asclepius appeared to the priest in a dream and said, 'Let that man keep his goods and go; he does not deserve even to have one eye.' The priest made inquiries about the man, and it emerged that this Cilician had had a wife with a daughter of her own by a previous marriage, and he had fallen in love with the girl and lived in open sin with her. But the mother caught them in bed and with a jab of her pin put out both of the girl's eyes and one of the man's.

11. In fact Apollonius gave a discourse on the subject of observing moderation in making a sacrifice or dedication. When a large number of people had gathered at the shrine soon after the expulsion of the man from Cilicia, Apollonius put some questions to the priest. 'Are the gods just?' he asked.

'Of course, entirely just,' was the reply.

'Are they wise too?'

'Why, more than anybody: it is their nature.'

'Do they know about human affairs, or are they ignorant of them?'

'That is the greatest difference between gods and men – men in their frailty do not even understand their own affairs, but the gods understand men's business as well as their own.'

'Very good answers,' said Apollonius to the priest, 'and very true. Well, since they understand everything, I think that a man who comes to a temple and has a good conscience should pray, "O gods, give me what I deserve." Since the pure naturally deserve good and the wicked evil, if the gods find a man to be honest and free from sin they are right to reward him, not with mere crowns of gold, but with every blessing, before they send him on his way. But if they see a man to be tainted and corrupt, they leave him to his fate, not showing their anger with him except for his effrontery in visiting a shrine without being pure.' And turning his eyes to the statue of Asclepius he said, 'It is your secret doctrine you practise, shared with no one else, Asclepius, when you forbid the wicked to approach here, even if they bring you all the wealth of India and Sardinia. They are not honouring heaven when they make these sacrifices and dedications; they are trying to avert judgement on themselves by means of bribes, but you gods in your great justice do not allow them to.' And he discoursed on many such subjects while he was still in his early youth.

12. The following story also concerns his stay in Aegae. The ruler of Cilicia was a brute and a pervert; and when he heard talk of Apollonius's youthful beauty he dropped the business he was doing, which was to hold court in Tarsus, and dashed off to Aegae, saying he was ill and needed the help of Ascle-

pius. There he approached Apollonius when he was walking
alone and said, 'Give me an introduction to the god.'

'Why do you need an introduction,' Apollonius replied,
'if you are good? The gods welcome honest men without a
recommendation.'

'Yes, Apollonius,' he said, 'but unlike me you have become
the god's friend.'

'It was my honesty that recommended me,' he replied,
'and because I practise it as best a young man can, I am
Asclepius's servant and companion. If you too care for goodness, don't be afraid to go before the god and pray for what
you want.'

'I will,' he replied, 'if I can pray to you first.'

'What prayer are you going to make to me?' Apollonius
asked.

'The prayer that one can only make to the beautiful – that
they be generous with their beauty and don't keep their
charms to themselves.'

As he said this he gave a languishing, misty-eyed look and
used all the motions of such unspeakable lechers. Apollonius
said with a scowl, 'You're mad, you scum.'

This not only made the man angry, but he threatened to
have Apollonius's head cut off. Apollonius laughed and
shouted the name of a certain day which was the third after
that one; on that day public slaves executed the brute on the
highway for conspiring against Rome with Archelaus the
King of Cappadocia.[8] This and many other stories have been
related by Maximus of Aegae, who was so admired as a

8. Archelaus died in A.D. 17, when his kingdom was incorporated as
a Roman province. Tiberius had a long history of bad relations with
him; and during the reign of Augustus, who died in A.D. 14, there had
been trouble with the Roman government. Archelaus's subjects had
brought accusations against him, including one of insanity. We are
told that at some point Augustus had even been obliged to install a
Roman official in Archelaus's kingdom.

speaker that he was put in charge of the emperor's correspondence.[9]

13. When Apollonius heard that his father had died, he hurried to Tyana and with his own hands laid him to rest near the tomb of his mother, who had died not long before. The estate, a wealthy one, he divided with his debauched and drunken brother, who was twenty-two and over the age for a guardian, while Apollonius being only twenty was subjected to guardians by the law. Then after staying again in Aegae, and making the shrine a Lyceum and an Academy, he returned to Tyana when he had reached man's estate and was master of his own property. When somebody told him that it was his duty to correct his brother and make him change his ways, he replied, 'It will look arrogant. How can I correct a person who is my senior? But I will do my best to cure him of these illnesses.' And so he gave him half of his own inheritance, saying that his brother needed more and he himself less. And when he had cleverly gained his attention and induced him to respond to correction, he said, 'Our father is no longer here to educate us and give us advice; you are all my family now, and of course I am yours. So if I do wrong, advise me and save me from error, and if you do wrong, allow me to point it out to you.' Thus, as people stroke restive and disobedient horses, he made his brother listen to persuasion and cured him of all his vices; previously he had been devoted to dice and drink, and had chased whores, priding himself on his hair (he actually used dyes on it) and strutting about in his vanity.

When Apollonius had settled matters with his brother, he next turned to his other relatives, and won over those of them that were in need by giving them the rest of his estate. He left only a little for himself, saying that when Anaxagoras of

9. Maximus's post was officially designated *ab epistulis graecis*. For more discussion of him, see the Introduction, p. 11 above.

Clazomenae let cattle and sheep have his land he was acting like a philosopher towards animals rather than men, and when Crates of Thebes threw his inheritance into the sea he had benefited neither men nor animals.

Now though Pythagoras was praised for his statement that a man should not have intercourse with any woman except his wife, Apollonius said that that commandment of Pythagoras applied to others, but he himself was not going to marry or have any sex at all. In this he surpassed the famous saying of Sophocles, who claimed that he had escaped an uncontrollable and harsh master when he reached old age;[10] for Apollonius's virtue and continence saved him from becoming a prey to that vice even as a boy, so that despite his youth and vigour he overcame sex and became master of the uncontrollable. In spite of this, sex is a subject on which some people slander him, claiming that he had an illicit affair and because of it spent a year away in the land of the Scythians, when the truth is that he never visited the Scythians once or was carried off by sexual passion. Even Euphrates does not slander him on sexual grounds in the mendacious attack that he wrote against him, as I will show when Euphrates comes into my story. The cause of their quarrel was that Apollonius kept rebuking him for doing everything for the sake of money, and tried to induce him not to be mercenary or sell his wisdom to the highest bidder. But I shall keep these details for their proper time.

14. Euxenus once asked Apollonius why he did not become a writer since his thoughts were so noble and his diction admirably forceful. 'Because I have not yet kept silence,' he answered. From then on he considered himself bound to silence, and held his tongue while his eyes and mind read and

10. This remark of Sophocles appears also in Plato's *Republic*, Book I (329C).

stored away many things in his memory.[11] In fact even when he was a hundred he surpassed Simonides himself in power of recollection; there is a hymn which he composed to Memory, and in it he says that time causes all things to pass away, but time itself is made ageless and immortal by memory. He was not sullen, however, during the time of his silence, but when addressed he replied with his eyes, his hands, or by motions of his head; and he did not seem gloomy or unsmiling, but retained his love of society and his agreeableness. He says that this way of life, which he practised for five whole years, was extremely difficult, because he could not speak when he had much to say, was forced not to listen when he heard much to make him angry, and often when he was inclined to correct somebody he used to say to himself, '"Be still, my soul," and tongue too,' and when people's conversation offended him he had to put off refuting them for the time being.

15. He spent the time of his silence partly in Pamphylia and partly in Cilicia, and though he travelled among such pleasure-loving peoples he never spoke and was not even induced to make a sound. Whenever a city he visited was in turmoil, as many were because of their worthless entertainments, he would simply enter; and by revealing his presence and showing through an expression or gesture the kind of rebuke he would like to administer, he would end all disturbance and reduce the people to silence as if at the Mysteries. But there is nothing wonderful about restraining people who are beginning to fight over dancers or horses, since those arguing over such matters can be made to blush and recover themselves and their senses by the sight of a true man. But when a city is

11. A similar vow of silence is attributed to a certain Secundus, a philosopher of the time of Hadrian (A.D. 117–38). The story of Secundus and the statements he wrote during the period of silence became widespread in late antiquity and the Middle Ages.

gnawed by famine it is no easy matter to win it over with calm and persuasive words and to check its fury. With Apollonius, however, even silence was enough to control those in such a condition.

For instance, he once came to Aspendus in Pamphylia, a city situated on the river Eurymedon, and the third in importance of the province. The inhabitants were actually buying vetch and living off anything that could feed them, because the grain was being held in store by the wealthy, who hoped that supplies of it would run out in the region. People of every age were infuriated with the chief magistrate and were lighting torches to burn him alive even though he clung to the statue of the emperor; these were then more feared and venerated than the statue of Zeus at Olympia, since the emperor was Tiberius,[12] and it is said that a man was held guilty of treason against him simply for hitting his own slave when the slave was carrying a silver drachma with Tiberius's image on it. So Apollonius approached the magistrate and by means of a gesture asked him what the matter was. The man said he was guilty of nothing, but he and the people alike were being wronged; and if he could not get a hearing he and they would share the same fate. Apollonius turned to the bystanders and nodded to them to listen. They not only fell silent out of reverence for him, but also put their torches on the altars nearby. So the magistrate plucked up his courage and named several people who, he said, were responsible for the present famine, since they had carried off the grain and were keeping it in different parts of the countryside. The people of Aspendus began to urge each other to go to these estates, but Apollonius by a motion of his head persuaded them not to, but rather to call the accused and recover the grain from them without pressure. When these came, he could scarcely restrain himself from breaking into speech against them, over-

12. Tiberius ruled A.D. 14–37.

come by the tears of the people – women and children had gathered, and the elderly were groaning as if they were going to die at any moment – but he obeyed his rule of silence, writing his reproach on a writing-tablet and giving it to the magistrate to read. The words were as follows: 'Apollonius to the corn-merchants of Aspendus. The earth in her justice is the mother of all, but you in your injustice have made her mother to yourselves alone, and if you do not stop I will not even let you remain upon her.' Frightened by his words, they flooded the market with grain, and the city was saved.

16. He also visited Antioch the Great when his silence was over,[13] and he went to the sanctuary of Apollo of Daphne. The Assyrians connect a well-known Arcadian myth with this place, saying that Daphne the daughter of Ladon was transformed there, and they have a river Ladon with a laurel growing beside it which they honour as the transfiguration of the girl. The shrine is encircled with cypresses of enormous height, and out of its soil come springs that flow silently and abundantly, in which Apollo is said to bathe. A young cypress-tree grows out of the ground there which they say was once an Assyrian youth called Cypress; the beauty of the tree makes the transformation plausible.

It may seem that I am beginning my story no better than a novice, inserting tales like this, but they are not here simply as tales. The point of my account is this. Apollonius saw that the sanctuary was pleasant but the visitors were entirely frivolous, being half-barbarian and uncultured. So he said, 'Apollo, change these dumb creatures into trees so that they can at least make some sound as cypresses.' After observing

13. This refers to Antioch in the Roman province of Syria; the site is modern Antakya. Nearby was the shrine of Apollo, which Philostratus himself had visited (as he tells us in the opening chapter of his *Lives of the Sophists*).

how calm the springs were, and how none of them splashed, he said, 'There is so little speech here that not even the fountains make a sound.' And looking at the Ladon he said, 'It is not only your daughter that was transformed, but you too, since you seem to have become a barbarian, instead of a Greek and an Arcadian too.'

When he was willing to converse, he avoided crowded and unruly places, saying that he needed the company of real men, and not mere humans. Instead he visited holy places and lived in any sanctuary to which entrance was permitted. When the sun came up he used to perform certain rites by himself, which he revealed only to those that had practised silence for four years; in the following hours, if he was in a Greek city and its cult was famous, he would call the priests and give them a discourse on the gods, setting them right if they had deviated from any of the traditional practices; but if the cult was foreign and peculiar, he would make inquiries about the founders and their purpose, and after finding out the reason for the customs and suggesting any improvement on the present practice he could think of, he would next go to his disciples and tell them to ask any questions they liked. For he held that those of his philosophy should converse with the gods as day broke but about them as it advanced, and thereafter they should discourse on human affairs. When he had answered all his disciples' questions and had had enough of such conversation, he would next go out to talk with anyone, which he never did until noon when the sun was at its zenith.

And when he had conversed as much as he thought enough, he would rub himself down with oil and then take a cold bath. For he called public baths 'men's senility'; when Antioch had been shut out of its baths as punishment for grave misconduct, he said, 'The emperor has rewarded your wickedness by giving you longer life.' And when the Ephesians

43

wanted to stone the chief magistrate for not heating the baths, he said, 'You blame the magistrate because you bathe in discomfort, but I blame you for bathing at all.'

17. The style of speech he adopted was not bombastic or swollen with artificial vocabulary, and yet not pedantic or over-Attic, since he considered a style more than moderately Attic uncouth. He was not given to logic-chopping or to long discourses, and he was never heard being ironic or crushing; when he answered he spoke as if inspired, saying 'I know,' 'I believe,' 'What are you all thinking of?' 'Let me tell you.' His sentences were short and polished, his words were simple and apt, and his sayings had the ring of commandments issued from a throne. When some babbler asked him why he did not inquire after knowledge, he replied, 'Because I inquired in my youth; now it is my duty not to inquire but to teach what I have found.' And when the man asked him next, 'How will a wise man converse?' he replied, 'Like a lawgiver: for a lawgiver must make ordinances for others out of his own beliefs.' This is how he conversed in Antioch, winning the admiration of completely uncultured folk.

18. After this he pondered making a greater journey, and decided on the country of India and the wise men there called Brahmans and Hyrcanians. He said that a young man ought to travel and be off to foreign parts. He considered the Magi that live in Babylon and Susa an extra dividend, for he would learn their ways too in the course of his journey. And so he revealed his decision to his disciples, who were seven in number, but they tried to urge some other plan in the hope of diverting him from this resolution. 'I,' he replied, 'have taken advice from the gods, and have told you my decision. I was testing you to see if you had the same strength as I do. But I see you are weak, so good-bye. I hope you remain

philosophers: but I must go where wisdom and my guardian spirit lead me.' So saying, he left Antioch with two servants he had inherited, one of whom was a shorthand writer and the other a secretary.

19. And so he arrived in ancient Nineveh, where there is an idol of barbarian type in the shape of Ino the daughter of Inachus, with little horns projecting from her temples and just breaking through. As Apollonius was staying there and showing more knowledge about the idol than the priests and the prophets, Damis of Nineveh came to hear him. This is the man whom I mentioned at the beginning as Apollonius's companion, who shared in all his wisdom and preserved many details about him. On this occasion, admiring him and eager to share his journey, he said, 'Let us go, Apollonius, you following God and I following you, for you might find me very useful. I may not know anything else, but I have been to Babylon; and, having made the journey recently, I know all the cities on the way and the villages, in which there are many attractions, and moreover I know every one of the barbarian languages. The Armenians have one, the Medes and Persians another, the Cadusians another, and I understand them all.' 'But I, my friend,' replied Apollonius, 'know them all, and have learned none.' The man from Nineveh was amazed, but Apollonius said, 'Do not be surprised if I know all that men say: I know all that men conceal too.' The Assyrian worshipped him when he said this, and regarded him as a spirit, and became his companion, growing in wisdom and remembering everything he learned.

The Assyrian's Greek was mediocre, for he lacked elegance of style, having been educated by barbarians, but he was very well able to record a discourse or a conversation, describing what he had heard or seen and making an account of such experiences, and he was better fitted to do this than anybody.

Damis's Scrap Book was composed for this reason: he did not want anything about Apollonius to go unknown, but wanted even his asides and random remarks to be recorded. The neat reply he made to a man who criticized this interest is worth noting. When some lazy and malevolent creature ridiculed him, saying that he was right to put down all Apollonius's sayings and opinions, but that in collecting all these trifling details he was acting like dogs when they feed on the scraps falling off the table at a feast, Damis replied, 'If the gods have a feast and dine together, they must certainly have attendants to make sure that even the bits of ambrosia that are dropped do not go to waste.' This was the kind of companion and admirer that Apollonius found as a travelling companion for most of his life.

20. When they were about to cross to Mesopotamia, the tax-collector stationed at Zeugma took them to the registry and asked them if they had anything to declare. 'Prudence,' replied Apollonius, 'Justice, Virtue, Temperance, Courage, Perseverance,' stringing together a lot of nouns all in the feminine gender. Immediately the official, with an eye to his own profit, said, 'Well then, make me a list of your slaves.' 'I cannot,' retorted Apollonius: 'it is not my slaves I am declaring, but my mistresses.'

Mesopotamia owes its existence to the Tigris and the Euphrates flowing from Armenia and the end of the Taurus range; these border a land mass that contains some cities but mostly villages. The Armenian and Arabian tribes which are cut off by these rivers are generally nomadic peoples; they are so convinced that they are islanders that they talk of going down to the sea when they approach the rivers, and consider the edge of the world to be the circle that these rivers form, for after curving around this land mass they enter the same sea. Some say that most of the Euphrates disappears into a marsh and that this river ends on land; others, telling an even less plausible story, say it flows below ground and rises in Egypt, mingling with the Nile.

To attain completeness and to leave out nothing that Damis wrote I would have liked to tell of their conversations as they travelled among these barbarians, but my narrative urges me on to a greater and more marvellous subject. However, I will not neglect these two points: the courage that Apollonius showed in travelling among barbarian tribes given to robbery and not yet subject to Rome, and the wisdom that enabled him even to attain understanding of the voices of animals, in the Arabian way. He even learnt this as he was travelling among those Arabs, who of all their nation are the most knowledgeable and skilful in this science. For it is common to all Arabs to listen to the prophecies of birds instead of oracles, and they understand dumb animals by eating the hearts of snakes, or (as some say) the livers.

. . . . .

27. When he arrived at Babylon, the official in charge of the great gates, learning that he had come as a sightseer, held out to him a golden statue of the king before which a person had to do obeisance, or he was forbidden to enter.[14] An ambassador from the Roman governor did not have to do this, but anyone coming from a barbarian land or touring the country is arrested in disgrace if he does not worship the statue first. Such are the silly duties the barbarians give to their officials. When Apollonius saw the statue, he asked, 'Who is this?' Hearing it was the king, he said, 'This man you do obeisance to will be well rewarded if I see that he is good and honest, and if I praise him for it.' So saying he passed through the

14. The ruling king in Babylon at this time was, as we learn later in the narrative, Vardanes, who ruled c. A.D. 41–5 (some scholars would, however, begin the reign c. 39, and some would end it c. 47).

gates. The official followed him in amazement, and taking hold of Apollonius's arm asked him through an interpreter his name, his family, his profession, and his purpose in coming; and after writing all this down in a note-book, as well as his clothing and appearance, he told Apollonius to wait.

28. Then he himself rushed off to the men they call the King's Ears,[15] and described Apollonius to them, warning them that he refused to do obeisance and was nothing like an ordinary human. They told him to bring Apollonius with respect and no rudeness of any sort, and when he had come, the oldest of them asked him what had induced him to disrespect the king. 'I have not disrespected him,' said Apollonius, 'yet.'

'Might you?' asked the other.

'Of course,' he replied, 'if on meeting him I find he is not good and honest.'

'What are the gifts you are bringing him?'

Apollonius again named Courage and Justice and so on, and the other said, 'Because you think he does not have them?'

'No,' replied Apollonius, 'because I think he will learn to use them if he has them.'

'Why,' came the reply, 'it was because he used them that he recovered this kingdom which you see (when others had lost it for him) and restored his house with much effort and vigour.'

'How many years is it since he recovered his power?' said Apollonius.

'It is two months since the third year began,' was the reply.

Apollonius then said with his usual loftiness, 'Bodyguard, or whatever your title is, Darius the father of Cyrus and Artaxerxes ruled this kingdom for sixty years or so, and then,

15. i.e. agents of the king. cf. the Persian King's 'Eye', parodied by Aristophanes in *Acharnians*, 92ff.

they say, suspecting that his end was near, sacrificed to justice saying, "O mistress, whoever you are," as if he had long desired justice but even then did not know what it was or think he possessed it. And he brought his sons up in such ignorance of it that they went to war with one another: one was wounded by his brother, and the other killed. But this king, who probably does not even know how to sit on his throne, you claim to be a model of all the virtues. You extol him, even though it is you that would profit, not I, if he became a better man.'

The barbarian looked at his neighbour and said, 'This man is a godsend that has been divinely brought here; by his good effect on a good man, he will make our king much better, much more moderate and gentle; I can see it in his appearance.' So they ran to spread the good news everywhere that there was a man standing at the King's doors who was wise, a Greek and full of excellent advice.

29. When the King received this message, he was just in the middle of sacrificing in the presence of the Magi (who superintend the performance of sacred rites). He called one of them and said, 'The fulfilment has come to the dream I described to you today when you attended my levée.' The king had in fact had this dream: he dreamt he was Artaxerxes the son of Cyrus and had changed into his shape, and he was now in terror that he might be overthrown by a revolution, since that was how he interpreted the change of shape. But when he heard the visitor was a Greek and a wise man, he was reminded of Themistocles of Athens, who had once come from the Greeks and stayed with Artaxerxes, esteeming the king as highly as the king esteemed him. And so the king stretched out his hand and said, 'Call him: it would be an excellent omen if he began by joining me in sacrifice and prayer.' [30.] So Apollonius was escorted in by a large crowd

who thought their attendance would be pleasing to the king when they heard of his joy at Apollonius's arrival.

Apollonius as he passed through the palace was not distracted by any of the famous sights, but passed them as if he were travelling a highway. Addressing Damis, he said, 'You were asking me the other day what the name was of the Pamphylian woman who is said to have been a companion of Sappho, and to have composed the hymns they sing to Artemis of Perge in a combination of Aeolian and Pamphylian styles.'

'I did ask you,' he replied, 'but you did not tell me her name.'

'No, my friend, but I expounded to you the melodies of the hymns and the references in them and how she adapted the Aeolian style to produce something uniquely and peculiarly Pamphylian. After that we went on to another subject and you forgot to ask me her name. Well, this skilful woman's name is Damophile, and they say that like Sappho she gathered a group of girls around her and composed poems, some of them love-poems and others hymns. The hymn to Artemis is partly her original composition and partly borrowed from those of Sappho.' How far he was from being daunted by the king and his pomp he revealed by not even thinking such things worth a glance: instead he talked about other things and no doubt did not even consider himself to be looking at the objects before him.

. . . . .

38. Once the king was about to go off to hunt the animals in the parks, in which the barbarians keep lions, bears and leopards. He asked Apollonius to join him in the hunt, but Apollonius replied, 'Have you forgotten, king, that I do not even join you when you sacrifice?[16] Besides it is no pleasure

16. In Chapters 31–2, omitted from this translation, Apollonius had refused to join Vardanes in making sacrifice.

to attack animals that are tortured and enslaved against their natures.' When the king asked him how he could make his power firm and safe, Apollonius replied, 'By honouring many and trusting few.'

The governor of Syria once sent him an embassy concerning two or more villages near Zeugma. He claimed that they had belonged long ago to Antiochus and Seleucus, but were now under his command, being the property of the Romans. The Arabians and Armenians, he said, did not harass them; but the king, though they were so far from him, enjoyed their revenues as if they belonged to him rather than to the Romans. The king sent the ambassadors out, and said, 'Apollonius, these villages were granted to my ancestors by the kings they mentioned, to maintain the animals which are caught in our country and sent to their side over the Euphrates. They are pretending to forget this and preparing some new aggression. What do you think the purpose of this embassy is?'

'It is moderate and reasonable, king,' he replied, 'since they prefer to obtain with your consent what they have the power to take without it, for the places are in their territory.' He added that it was a mistake to quarrel with the Romans over villages which were probably smaller than some owned by private citizens, and a mistake in fact even to start a war with them over a large issue.

When the king fell ill, Apollonius attended him and gave so many inspired discourses on the soul that the king recovered and said to his attendants, 'Apollonius has made me indifferent not only to my kingdom but even to death.'

39. Once the king was showing him the tunnel under the Euphrates, and said, 'What do you think of this achievement?' But Apollonius, showing his contempt for artifice, said, 'It would be a real achievement, king, if your people could wade

through such a deep and turbulent river.' When the king showed him the walls of Ecbatana and claimed they were the work of gods, Apollonius said, 'They are certainly not the work of gods, and perhaps not of true men either, since the city in which the Spartans live, king, has no walls.'

Moreover, when the king had heard a dispute between some villages and was boasting to Apollonius that he had listened to the case for two days, he said, 'You took a long time to find where justice was.'

A lot of money had once come to the king from his subjects and he opened his treasury, showing Apollonius his money and trying to tempt him to desire wealth. But Apollonius did not express wonder at anything he saw, saying only, 'This is money to you, king, but rubbish to me.'

'Well, what is the best way for me to use it?'

'Spend it,' was the reply, 'for you are a king.'

40. After such conversations with the king, whom he found eager to take his advice, and after he had had enough of conversing with the Magi, he said, 'Come, Damis, let us start out for India. Those who landed among the Lotus-Eaters were seduced by the food away from their native ways, and we must have tasted something here to make us loiter for longer than the right and proper time.'

'I fully agree,' said Damis, 'but thinking of the time which you saw prophesied by the lioness,[17] I have been waiting for it to be completed, and it has not yet all passed, as we have been here a year and four months. Could we start now without mishap?'

'The king will not let us go, Damis,' he replied, 'before

17. In Chapter 22, omitted from this translation, Apollonius had come upon the corpse of a pregnant lioness that proved to be carrying eight whelps. He deduced from this portent that the length of his stay at Babylon would be one year and eight months.

the last four months are past; you see he is a virtuous man and too good to be a ruler of barbarians.'

41. But when he finally had decided to leave and the king had at last permitted him to go, Apollonius remembered the gifts that he had asked to be deferred until he had found friends there, and he said, 'Good king, I have not yet given my host any present and I owe the Magi a fee. Please take care of them and for my sake be kind to them, because they are wise and very loyal to you.'

The king was delighted, and said, 'Tomorrow you will see them envied and highly honoured. But since you want none of my property, at least let these' (he pointed to Damis and the others) 'receive money from me and whatever else they like.'

But when they too declined this offer, Apollonius said, 'You see, king, how many hands I have and how like each other they are.'

'Well, take a guide anyhow,' said the king, 'and camels to ride on. The journey is too great to be done entirely on foot.'

'As you wish, king. They say the journey is impossible without such transport, and moreover they are animals easy to feed, even where there is no fodder. I also think we must take water and carry it in skins like wine.'

'The land is waterless for three days,' said the king, 'but after that rivers and springs are numerous. You must take the Caucasus road, on which supplies are abundant and the country is friendly.'

The king asked Apollonius what he was going to bring back to him from the people there, and he said, 'A fine gift, king. If their company makes me wiser, I will come back to you a better man than I am now.'

The king embraced him at these words, and said, 'Come back: that will be a great gift in itself.'

BOOK II

1. The party and its guide set out from Babylon in summer-time on their mounts, with a groom for the camels and plenty of supplies, given by the king, for their every need. The land through which they were travelling was fertile, too; and they received an elaborate welcome from every village, since the leading camel had a chain of gold on its forehead to advise all in their path that this was a friend of the king and provided for by him.

. . . . .

17. When they had reached the Indus and were preparing to cross it, they asked their Babylonian guide if he had had any experience of the river, in the hope of information about the crossing. He said that he had never sailed on it before, and in fact did not know at what point the crossing was made.

'Why didn't you hire a guide, then?' they asked.

'We have a guide,' he answered, revealing a letter designed for the purpose. This, it seems, really made them admire the courtesy and thoughtfulness of Vardanes, as he had sent this letter to the viceroy of the Indus who was not, however, subject to him. In it Vardanes reminded him of a benefit. He said he would not ask a return for that, because it was not in his nature to ask a return for favours; but he would be grateful if the viceroy welcomed Apollonius and provided for him. He had also given money to the guide to give to Apollonius if he noticed him in any need, so that he would not have to depend on another's generosity.

When the Indian received the letter, he said that he felt greatly honoured, and would be as attentive to Apollonius as if the King of India had written on his behalf. He gave him the vice-regal ship to cross in and other boats in which the camels were ferried over, as well as a guide for the whole region which the Hydraotes borders. He also wrote to his own king, advising him to prove as good as Vardanes to a man who was both a Greek and under divine protection.

18. They crossed the Indus at a width of about five miles: so great is its navigable size. In their account of this river, they relate that it rises in the Caucasus, already larger at its source than any single river in Asia, and as it progresses it absorbs other navigable rivers. Acting like the Nile, it floods India, silting the land and allowing the Indians to sow in the same way as the Egyptians. I hardly dare contradict the authorities that vouch for the snows of Ethiopia and the Mountains of the Cataract,[1] but I cannot agree with them when I consider that the Indus behaves as the Nile does without snow falling in the region of its origin. Besides, I am certain that the divine purpose has made Ethiopia and India the promontories of the entire earth, and causes those in the farthest east and the farthest west to be black: and how could that happen to them unless they had summer even in winter? And if a land is warmed by the sun throughout the year, how could it conceivably have snow? And how could the snow be

1. Herodotus also reports and rejects the theory that the risings of the Nile were due to its origins in the mountain snows of Ethiopia: II. 22. The theory seems to go back to the philosopher Anaxagoras in the fifth century B.C. In modern times it was once considered as very near to the truth, but it now appears that melting snows have nothing to do with the risings of the Nile. They are caused by the heavy summer rains on the Ethiopian plateau. For a full and fascinating discussion, cf. Danielle Bonneau, *La crue du Nil: divinité égyptienne* (1964).

sufficient to make the rivers there rise above their banks? And even if snow fell in such tropical regions, how could it create such a flood when it melted? And how could it be enough for a river that floods all of Egypt?

19. As they crossed the river, they say, they observed many hippopotamuses and many crocodiles, as those who sail the Nile do. They say also that there are flowers in the Indus similar to those that grow in the Nile, that the climate in India is warm in winter and stifling in summer, and that it has been so well constituted by heaven that there is constant rain there. Also they were apparently told by the Indians that the king visited the river in the right season and sacrificed to it black bulls and horses – black being more highly regarded by the Indians than white, I suppose, because of their own colour. After his sacrifice he would throw into the river a golden measure, which resembled those used for measuring grain. The Indians had no notion why the king did this; but the party inferred that this measure was thrown in to ensure either plentiful harvest, which farmers 'measure' out, or else a 'measured' flow, so that the river should not come down in spate and swamp the land.

20. When they had crossed the river, the guide from the viceroy led them straight to Taxila where the Indian king had his palace. They say that those on the other side of the Indus wore the local linen, shoes of bark, and hats for the rain, while the upper class dressed in cotton. This, they relate, grows on a tree with a trunk like a poplar but leaves like a willow. Apollonius says he was pleased by the cotton, since it looked like a grey philosopher's cloak. In fact, the cotton is exported from India to many of the shrines in Egypt.

Taxila is apparently similar to Nineveh in size, symmetrically fortified like a Greek city, and is the capital of the king who ruled Porus's domain at the time.[2] They say they saw a temple in front of the walls a little less than a hundred feet in length and made of stone covered with stucco.[3] Inside it there was a shrine comparatively small for such a large, many-columned temple, but worth admiring. On every wall there are fixed bronze panels illustrating the deeds of Alexander and Porus. On them, in orichalc, silver, gold and bronze, there are drawn elephants, horses, soldiers, helmets and shields, with spears, javelins and swords all in iron. A famous picture, for example one by Zeuxis, Polygnotus or Euphranor, is praised because the artists liked effects of shadow, vividness, and contrasts of emphasis; and the same effects are apparently to be observed in these pictures where the materials are blended like colours. The purpose of the pictures also pleased them. Porus had dedicated them after the death of the Macedonian, but even so the Macedonian is shown as the victor, winning the wounded Porus over and giving him India after he had conquered it. Porus is also said to have mourned Alexander at his death and grieved for him as a good and noble king; and while Alexander lived he is said never to have spoken as a king, though Alexander allowed him, or to have given orders to Indians; but like a viceroy he was entirely moderate and did everything to please his friend.

21. My account forbids me to omit the records of this Porus. When the Macedonian was about to cross, some were advising Porus to make allies of those across the Hyphasis and the

2. Porus was the great Indian king who resisted Alexander the Great. At the time of Apollonius's visit the king was Gondophares. Modern excavations at Taxila have shown that Philostratus's account of the city is substantially accurate: cf. Sir John Marshall, *A Guide to Taxila*, 4th edn, 1960, pp. 28–30.

3. This temple has been recognized at Taxila: it is the temple of Jaṇḍiāl (*ibid.*, pp. 29 and 88–9).

Ganges, saying that Alexander would not dare to confront an entirely united India. Porus replied: 'If my kingdom is such that it cannot be saved without allies, it would be better not to be king.' When the news came that Darius had been captured, he called him 'the Great King, but no man'. When the groom had prepared the elephant on which he was to fight, and said to him, 'This will carry you, king', he replied, 'No, I will carry it, if I prove a man worthy of myself.' Advice was given to him to sacrifice to the river and pray that it should not bear the rafts of the Macedonians or allow Alexander to sail, but he said, 'It is not for men in arms to curse.' And after the battle, when he had shown Alexander how godlike he was and of more than mortal nature, one of his relatives said to him, 'Porus, if you had done obeisance when Alexander crossed, you would not have suffered defeat in battle, or lost so many Indians, or received a wound yourself.' He replied: 'I had heard of Alexander's nobility, and I foresaw that, if I made obeisance, he would think me a slave, but if war, a king. I preferred to be admired rather than pitied, and I was not disappointed. I proved myself the man Alexander saw me to be, and so in one day I lost and gained everything.' This is the character the Indian is reputed to have had. He is also said to have been outstanding among Indians for his handsomeness and height, which was greater than that of any man since those at Troy; and he was very young when he fought Alexander.

22. Apollonius spent what turned out to be a long time in this temple until the king could be informed that visitors had arrived. In the meanwhile he said, 'Damis, does figurative art have intrinsic value?'

'Yes,' said Damis, 'if truth does.'

'What does this kind of art do?'

'It blends all the colours there are, blue with green, white with black, red with yellow.'

'Why does it blend them?' asked Apollonius, 'since it is not simply for ostentation, like cosmetics.'

'To achieve imitation,' Damis replied, 'to reproduce dogs, horses, humans, ships, everything under the sun. In fact artists sometimes represent the sun himself with his four horses, which is the way he appears in these regions, I believe; and sometimes again blazing in heaven, when artists represent the heavens and the home of the gods.'

'So figurative art is imitation, Damis?'

'Of course,' was the reply; 'if that was not its business, it would be considered absurd, a pointless mixing of colours.'

'Now,' said Apollonius, 'the things we see in the sky, when the clouds are separated from one another, centaurs and goat-deer, and wolves and horses for that matter – how do you account for them? As the products of imitation, I presume?'

'I suppose so,' Damis said.

'Then is god an artist, Damis? Does he leave the winged chariot in which he travels setting the affairs of gods and men to right, and sit on these occasions drawing these things for fun, like children in sand?'

Damis blushed, when his argument proved to come to such an absurd conclusion. Apollonius did not embarrass him, for he never pressed his questions, but said, 'Surely what you mean, Damis, is that the things that pass through the sky are shapeless and haphazard as far as god is concerned, but we, because imitation is in our nature, depict and create them?'

'Yes,' said Damis, 'that is the belief we should hold, Apollonius: it is more plausible and far sounder.'

'Well then, imitation is of two kinds, Damis. Let us hold that one kind is imitation of both the hand and the mind, and this is figurative art, and the other is drawing with the mind alone.'

'It is not of two kinds,' said Damis. 'The one kind we should consider more perfect, the figurative, which can draw both with the mind and the hand, whereas the other is a part of the first, since you can comprehend and copy things in the mind without being an artist, but you could not use your hand to represent them.'

'Because your hand was maimed by an injury or disease, Damis?'

'No, but because you had never handled any kind of brush or tool or colour, and were completely ignorant of drawing.'

'Well, Damis,' said Apollonius, 'we are both agreed that imitative art is given to men by nature, but figurative art by skill, and the same would appear to be true of plastic art. But, to take portraiture, I don't think you consider it merely the art of using colours, since early painters practised it contentedly with only one colour; as it advanced it involved four and then more colours. Line-drawing and the technique that avoids colour, using only light and shade, deserve to be called painting too, since in such productions we can see similarity, shape, intelligence, modesty, boldness, although they lack colours and do not show blood or the colour of a person's hair or beard; being composed in one colour, they do not distinguish a fair-haired man from a white-haired one. If we draw one of these Indians even with a white chalk, he will obviously seem black; the snub nose, fuzzy hair, large jaws and (so to speak) bulging eyes have a black effect on the thing seen, and portray an Indian, to an educated observer at any rate. I would say, then, that those who view the works of figurative art, need imitative art, since no one is likely to praise the picture of a horse or bull if he has not a conception of the creature portrayed; no one is likely to admire Timomachus's Ajax, whom the artist represents as insane, if he does not recall to his mind the image of Ajax and how he is likely to have looked after killing the cattle at Troy, sitting in despair and planning suicide. But these ingenious pictures of Porus's, Damis, we should not define merely as works of metal-casting, since they look like pictures, or as works of representation, since they are the creations of one man who combined the arts of representation and metal-working, just as in Homer Hephaestus is supposed to have done with the shield of Achilles. These pictures too are full of men "killing and being killed",[4] and one would say that the ground was smeared with blood, even though it is of bronze.'

23. As Apollonius was giving this discourse, messengers arrived from the king with an interpreter, announcing that he would have Apollonius as his guest for three days, since it was not lawful for strangers to stay in the city longer; and they led the way to the palace. I have mentioned what the walls of the city were like; the party says that it was a tangle of narrow streets, like Athens, and the houses were so built that from the outside they appeared to be of only one storey, but when you went inside they proved to be subterranean, with the same plan below ground as above.

24. They say there was also a shrine of the Sun, with Ajax the elephant pasturing in it, and statues of Alexander in gold and others of Porus which were of dark bronze.[5] The walls of the shrine were of red stone that had a golden sheen, giving off a light like the sun's rays. The image itself was of mother-of-pearl, made in the symbolic shape that all barbarians use for their holy objects.

25. In the palace they apparently saw no elaborate rooms, no bodyguard or watchmen, but just as in the houses of the upper class there were a few slaves and three or four people awaiting an audience with the king. They say they admired this

4. The shield: *Iliad* XVIII. 483ff. The quotation is from *Iliad* IV. 451.
5. This shrine has been recognized in the excavations at Taxila by the discovery of a stone statue of the Sun-god (Marshall, *op. cit.*, p. 30).

simplicity more than the splendour of Babylon, and even more so when they went inside, since it seems that the men's quarters and the colonnades and the whole forecourt were plain.[6]

26. Apollonius concluded that the Indian was a philosopher and, with the interpreter beside him, he said, 'I am glad, king, to see that you are a philosopher.'

'I am very glad,' he replied, 'that you think me so.'

'Is this the custom with you,' said Apollonius, 'or did you introduce this moderation into your kingdom?'

'Our customs are modest, and I observe them even more modestly,' he replied. 'I have more than any man, but need little, for all my friends' possessions I consider mine.'

'Your wealth is enviable,' said Apollonius, 'if you value your gold and silver less than your friends, from whom you derive many advantages.'

'Why,' he said, 'I give my enemies a share of my riches too. There are always barbarians hostile to my country, who make incursions across my borders, so I win them over with this money and they guard my country. They both avoid raiding my possessions and keep out their barbarian neighbours, who are unmanageable.'

Apollonius asked him if Porus too had paid them money. 'Porus,' he said, 'loved war: I love peace.'

Apollonius was quite won over by these remarks, and was so struck by him that once, when he was rebuking Euphrates for not acting like a philosopher, he said, 'But let us at least respect the Indian Phraotes' (since that was his name).

A viceroy who had been greatly favoured by him wanted to present him with a golden crown studded with precious stones, but he said, 'Even if I were one of those who covet

6. Excavations have confirmed Philostratus's report of the modest proportions of the palace at Taxila (*ibid.*, pp. 30 and 69).

such things, I would have declined it now and torn it from my head in the presence of Apollonius; but since I never saw fit to wear such crowns before, how could I use ornaments now, mistaking my guest and forgetting myself?'

Apollonius also asked him about his diet and he said, 'Of wine I drink as much as I sacrifice to the Sun. What I catch in the hunt others eat: the exercise is enough for me. My food is vegetables, the centre of date-palms and their fruit[7] and everything that grows beside the river. I also eat many things that grow on trees: they are harvested by these hands of mine.' Apollonius was delighted when he heard this, and kept glancing at Damis.

27. When they had had enough conversation about the journey to the Brahmans, the king gave orders for the guide from the king of Babylon to be entertained, as was his custom, and dismissed the guide from the viceroy with provisions for the road. He took Apollonius's hand, and after telling the interpreter to go away, he said, 'Will you invite me to drink?' asking him in Greek.

Apollonius was stunned, and said, 'Why didn't you talk this way from the beginning?'

'I was afraid,' said the king, 'to appear forward and forget myself and the barbarian birth that fate has allotted me. But I was overcome when I saw you were pleased with me, and could not conceal my true self, and will fully satisfy you that I am thoroughly grounded in Greek.'

'Well then,' said Apollonius, 'why didn't you invite me to dinner yourself instead of asking me to invite you?'

'Because I think you are superior to me,' he said, 'since there is something more kingly in wisdom.' At the same time, he led Apollonius and his party to the place where he usually

7. The translator and the editor consider the words 'and their fruit' an interpolated gloss.

bathed. His bathing-place was a park about an eighth of a mile long. In the middle there was dug a pool into which flowed springs of warm, fresh water; on either side there were spaces in which the king practised the javelin and the discus in the Greek way: he was strong in body both because of his age, being twenty-seven, and because he took this exercise. Whenever he was tired of that, he would jump into the water and exercise himself by swimming. When they had bathed, they proceeded to the dining-room wearing wreaths, since that is the custom of the Indians when they go to the palace to drink.

28. It would not be right to omit the arrangement of the feast either, since Damis has described it in detail. The king takes his ease on a couch with no more than five of his close kin, while all the rest sit on chairs to dine. There is a table built in the middle like an altar about the height of a man's knee, and with a circumference as large as a circle of thirty men holding hands. On it are strewn branches of laurel and others which resemble laurel, but in India produce perfume, and there are set out fish, fowl, whole lions, venison, boar and loins of tiger (they avoid eating the other parts of this animal, since they say that as soon as it is born it raises its front paws to the rising sun). The guest gets up, goes to the table, and taking or carving what he likes, goes back to his chair and eats his fill, with a lot of bread as well.

When they are satisfied, bowls of silver and gold are carried in, each one enough for ten guests, and they drink from them putting their heads down like animals at water. While they are drinking, shows of skill are brought on which are dangerous and quite serious. A boy, like the member of a dancing-troop, jumped lightly about while an arrow was shot at the same time into the air, and when it was at the highest point of its path the boy leapt up, making a somersault over the arrow, with the certainty of being hit if he missed his leap, since the archer before shooting went round the diners showing the point and letting them test the arrow. Shooting through a sling, using a hair as a target, and drawing an outline of one's own son in arrows while he stands against a board are others of their convivial pursuits, and they do them successfully even when drunk.

. . . . .

40. When the dispute had been settled,[8] Apollonius approached the Indian and said, 'This is the third of the days, king, in which you were to make me your guest. At dawn tomorrow I must leave as the law commands.'

'No,' he said, 'you are not at odds with the law yet. You can stay tomorrow too, since you arrived in the afternoon.'

'I appreciate your present,' said Apollonius, 'as you seem to be stretching the law for my benefit.'

'I only wish,' he replied, 'that for you I could break it. But tell me, Apollonius, the camels which I am told you are travelling on, they have brought you from Babylon, haven't they?'

'Yes,' said Apollonius, 'Vardanes gave us them.'

'Will they be able to carry you on again, then, when they have already come so many miles from Babylon?'

Apollonius did not answer, but Damis said, 'My master has no conception of this journey, or of the tribes among which we are going to be. He supposes we will find others like you and Vardanes everywhere, and that reaching India is child's play. As for the camels, he does not admit to you what state they are in; they are in such bad condition that they are being carried by us rather than the other way round, and we need others. If they collapse in some deserted place in

8. In the preceding chapter, omitted here, Apollonius advised the king in a case being tried before him.

India, we will sit fending vultures and wolves off them, and no one will fend them off us, because we will die too.'

So the king answered, 'I will remedy that. I will give you new ones – you need four, I think – and the viceroy guarding the Indus will send four others to Babylon, since I have a herd of entirely white camels by the Indus.'

'Perhaps, king,' said Damis, 'you would give us a guide too.'

'Of course,' he replied, 'with a camel and provisions, and I will write to Iarchas, the senior philosopher, so that he will welcome Apollonius as a man fully as virtuous as himself, and you as lovers of wisdom and the companions of an inspired man.'

The Indian also offered them money, precious stones, linen, and other such things in huge amounts, but Apollonius said, 'I have enough money, since Vardanes gave some secretly to the guide; but I will take the linen, since it resembles a philosopher's cloak of the old-fashioned, genuine Attic kind.' He also took one of the stones and said, 'You excellent stone, you have come to me at the right time and with a god's help.' I suppose he had discerned some mysterious, divine power in it. Damis and the others refused money, but helped themselves to plenty of the precious stones, planning to dedicate them to the gods when they returned to their own countries.

41. When they had stayed there the next day too, since the Indian did not want to part with them, he gave them his letter to Iarchas, which ran as follows:

'King Phraotes greets his teacher Iarchas and Iarchas's companions.

'Apollonius, a very wise man, thinks you wiser than himself, and is coming to learn your lore. When he leaves you, make sure he knows all that you do. He will not forget any of your lessons, since his memory is as extraordinary as his conversation. Let him see the throne on which I sat when you gave me my kingdom, father Iarchas. His companions also deserve praise for their devotion to so great a man. Good-bye, Iarchas. Good-bye, all of you.'

42. When they had left Taxila and gone two days' journey, they came to the plain in which Alexander is said to have fought Porus, and apparently they saw gates there which did not enclose anything but were built as a trophy. On top of them there was dedicated a statue of Alexander riding an eight-horse chariot, the way he stood when he conquered the viceroys of Darius at Issus. In fact there are said to be two sets of gates, not far from one another, one bearing Porus and the other Alexander, represented as they met after the battle, I suppose, since one of them appears in a gesture of greeting, and the other in a gesture of submission.

43. When they had passed the Hydraotes and passed several tribes, they came to the Hyphasis. About four miles past this they found altars with this inscription:

'To my father Ammon, my brother Hercules, Athene of Forethought, Olympian Zeus, the Cabiri of Samothrace, the Sun of India, and Apollo of Delphi.'

They say there was also a bronze tablet dedicated there with the legend, 'Alexander stopped here.' We must conclude that the altars were set up by Alexander to commemorate the limits of his empire, while I suppose the tablet was dedicated by the Indians across the Hyphasis to celebrate the fact that Alexander advanced no further.

BOOK III

1. You should first know the size of the Hyphasis as it crosses India and its remarkable features. This river rises from a level plain and is navigable from its source, though as it goes on it becomes unfit for boats: spits of rock jut from each bank in turn, rising out of the water, and the current as it twists around them naturally makes the river unnavigable. In breadth it equals the Danube, which is considered the largest river in Europe. Trees of a corresponding size grow along the banks, giving off a kind of balm which the Indians use as a marriage perfume: if the guests omit to sprinkle this perfume on the couple, the ceremony is considered incomplete and contracted without the favour of Aphrodite. They say that the trees in the area of the river are dedicated to this goddess; and so are the famous peacock-fish, which do not breed anywhere else. They have been given the same name as the bird because of their blue dorsal fins, spotted scales, and golden tail-fins which they can spread at will. Another creature in this river resembles a white worm, and is melted down to produce an oil. The flame given off by this oil can be resisted by nothing but glass. Only the king may catch the animal, and he uses it for taking cities, for as soon as its fat touches the parapets it bursts into a flame which is too strong for any of the anti-incendiary devices yet invented.

2. The famous wild asses are apparently also caught in the marshes here. These creatures have a horn on their foreheads with which they fight as bulls do, and quite courageously. The Indians make the horns into cups, and whoever drinks from

one of these cups cannot fall ill that day or feel pain if he is wounded; he can pass through fire and is immune against drugs that are usually poisonous. These cups are the king's private property and he alone is allowed to hunt the animal. Apollonius says he saw the creature and admired its qualities, but when Damis asked him if he believed the story about the cup, he replied, 'I will, if I hear that the king of the Indians in this region is immortal. The man who can offer me or anybody else so fortifying and healthy a drink must surely have it served to himself too, and drink from this horn every day to the point of intoxication. I hardly think anyone will condemn getting drunk on this.'

3. They also met a woman there, it seems, who was black from the top of her head to her breasts and completely white from her breasts to her feet. While the others thought she was a monster and fled, Apollonius took her by the hand, realizing what she was: for in fact such women in India are considered sacred to Aphrodite, and multicoloured women are born to serve the goddess, like Apis in Egypt.

4. From there they record that they crossed the Caucasus where it stretches down to the Red Sea.[1] The mountain is covered with spice-bearing trees. On the spurs there grows cinnamon, which looks like the tendrils of a vine but is identified by means of nanny-goats. If you offer cinnamon to one, it will nuzzle your hand like a dog and as you go away it will follow, burying its nose in the shrub; if the goatherd leads it off it will wail as if it had been torn away from a lotus-plant. On the precipices of the mountain, however, grow frankincense trees and many other kinds too, including pepper-trees

---

1. The odd-sounding geography, which echoes II. 2 (omitted in this translation), refers apparently to the mountains between the Hyphasis and the Ganges.

which are cultivated by monkeys. Since the party found room to record what the trees looked like I shall give their description. The pepper-tree looks like the Greek willow in every respect, down to the clusters of fruit, except that it grows on precipices and is inaccessible to man. But a tribe of monkeys lives there in the crannies and hollows of the mountain, and the Indians value them so highly that they use dogs and weapons to keep lions away from the animals when they are biting off the peppers. Lions attack the monkeys for two reasons, either to get a cure when they are ill, for monkeys' flesh arrests their diseases, or to get food when they are old: being past the age for hunting deer and boar, they use their remaining strength to prey on the monkeys, while the humans, feeling themselves indebted to the monkeys, intervene by taking up arms to defend them against the lions. But the method used for the peppers is this. The Indians make their way to the trees lower down, pick the fruit, and gather it into little round clearings which they make near the trees, pretending to dump it as if it were worthless and of no serious use to humans. The monkeys watch from their inaccessible places above, and when night comes they imitate the actions of the Indians by tearing the clusters of fruit from the trees and bringing them to the clearings, where they dump them. The next morning the Indians carry off the piles of spice without having done any work, in fact having got them during their leisure hours and even while they slept.

5. After crossing the mountain they apparently saw a level plain divided up by ditches fed from the Ganges and full of water, some of them running at right angles and others diagonally. As well as providing boundaries these are used to irrigate the plain when the soil is thirsty. The soil here is the best in India and the region is the largest of its divisions, since it takes fifteen days to cross it to the Ganges and eighteen to

cross it from the sea to the mountain of the monkeys, which it skirts. The whole area is flat, with dark soil that can grow anything. They saw stalks of corn standing as tall as bulrushes on it, beans three times larger than the Egyptian kind, and sesame and millet, all of it enormous. They also saw those nuts which are often dedicated in our temples as freaks. The vines, however, are small, like those in Lydia and Maeonia, but the wine they produce is drinkable and of a fine bouquet from the time of vintage. They also came across a tree there like a laurel, bearing a fruit resembling a huge pomegranate, and the centre inside the husk was as blue as the flowers of the bluebell and sweeter than any other thing the seasons produce.

6. As they came down the mountain, they apparently witnessed a snake-hunt. I must describe this, because those who are addicted to such things have given long accounts of the hare, with descriptions and advice for hunting it; and it would be extremely foolish of me to omit the story of a bold and amazing hunt, a story moreover which was included by the man in whose honour I am writing. All the countryside of India is infested by snakes of enormous length; the marshes and the mountains are full of them, no hill is free from them. The marsh variety is sluggish, with a length of sixty feet; they have no hood, but resemble female snakes. They are very dark-backed, and less scaly than other kinds. Homer approaches closer than most poets to a true description of them when he describes the snake that lived near the fountain at Aulis as 'of russet back',[2] while other poets describe the related snake in the Nemean wood as having a crest, something not to be found in marsh snakes.

7. The snakes from the foothills and the ridges seek their prey on the plains. They are in every way superior to the marsh

2. *Iliad* II. 308.

variety; they grow to greater length, move faster than the swiftest rivers, and nothing escapes them. These do have a crest, which is of moderate size when they are young, but increases as they reach maturity until it grows to a great height while the snakes turn crimson and develop serrated backs. These grow beards too and display their throats with scales glittering like silver. Their eyeballs are flashing stones which apparently have an extraordinary power for many secret purposes. The snake of the plains is a choice catch for hunters when it is dragging off an elephant, because that is fatal for both. Those who capture snakes also prize the eyes, the skin and the teeth. These are in every respect like the tusks of the largest boars, except that they are lighter, of spiral shape and with a permanent sharpness like those of the largest fish.

8. The mountain-snakes have scales of golden appearance: they are of greater length than the plain-variety, and have bushy beards, which are also golden. They have more prominent eyebrows than the plain-variety, and under the eyebrow a terrible eye with an unwavering glare. They also make a sound rather like clashing bronze when they burrow underground, and from their crests, which are crimson, there gleams a fire brighter than a torch. These also catch elephants, and the way they are caught by the Indians is this. The Indians weave golden letters into a scarlet cloth, and put it in front of the snake's hole, after casting a spell of sleep on the letters. This captivates the unmoving eye of the snake, and the Indians also recite much of their secret magic over it, which brings it out and makes it raise its head out of the hole and go to sleep over the letters. Then the Indians attack it where it lies with axe blows, and after cutting off the head extract the stones from it. And they say that in the head of the mountain-snake there are hidden stones of many hues, giving off every colour,

and having a magic power like the ring that Gyges is said to have had.[3] But often the snake seizes the Indian despite his axe and his magic, and carries him off into its hole, almost making the mountain shake. These snakes are also said to inhabit the mountains around the Red Sea, where they apparently make a terrible hissing, and come down to the shore to swim far out into the deep. The age of the creature, however, is impossible to discover, and I would not be believed if I told it. That is all I know about snakes.

9. The city below the mountain is very large, and apparently called Paraca. In the centre of it there are dedicated many snakes' heads, since the Indians of that region practise that kind of hunting from their youth. They are said also to understand the speech and advice of animals by eating either the heart or the liver of a snake. As the party went on it evidently heard the pipe of some herdsman calling his herd, and he turned out to be pasturing white deer. The Indians milk these, considering their milk nutritious.

10. From there they travelled for four days through rich, well-tilled country before nearing the Wise Men's hill. But their guide ordered his camel to kneel, and jumped off it terrified and sweating profusely. Apollonius realized where they had arrived, and said, laughing at the Indian's fear, 'Even if this man had sailed into harbour after crossing a wide sea, I think, he would be distressed by land and fear being in port.' With these words he made his camel crouch, as he was by now used to giving such orders. What caused the guide such terror was the proximity of the Wise Men, since the Indians fear them even more than their own king. In fact the king himself who rules the country asks the advice of these men on every subject, what to say and what to do, like a man con-

3. The ring of Gyges could make him invisible: cf. Herodotus I. 8.

sulting a god; and they signify what he would do well to do, and discourage and warn him against what he would not.

11. They were about to put up in the nearby village, which is less than a few hundred yards from the Wise Men's hill, when they saw, it appears, a young man running towards them. He was a particularly dark Indian, but with a bright crescent-shaped mark on his forehead. I gather that the same thing appeared many years later in Meno, who was an Ethiopian and the ward of the sophist Herodes,[4] but as he entered manhood this white mark faded and vanished with his youth. The Indian, it seems, carried a golden anchor, which is a customary token of messengers in India since it 'secures' everything.

12. He ran up to Apollonius and greeted him in Greek, which was not in itself surprising since everybody in the village talked Greek. But his saying 'Hello' to each of them by name amazed all of them except Apollonius; he felt assured of his mission, because he looked at Damis and said, 'We really have come to wise men, since they seem to have foreknowledge.' Immediately he asked the Indian what he had to do, being eager to meet them. The Indian said, 'These men you must leave here, but you must yourself come immediately because the Masters invite you.' [13.] The word 'Masters' in itself seemed Pythagorean to Apollonius, and he followed gladly.

The hill where the Wise Men have their settlement is apparently about the height of the Acropolis at Athens, though it rises sheer from a plain, and it is similarly defended by natural rock on every side. In many parts of this rock there

4. In his *Lives of the Sophists* Philostratus included a lengthy biography of the Athenian sophist Herodes Atticus: in it he mentions Meno again.

could be seen prints of cloven hooves and shapes of beards, faces and also backs as if people had fallen down. It seems that Dionysus tried to take the place along with Hercules, and asked the Pans to attack it, thinking they were well suited for a sudden attack. They, however, were crazed by the Wise Men and fell everywhere, and the rocks seemed to be shaped to represent their crime. Around the rock they apparently saw a cloud inside which the Indians live, visible or invisible as they please. But the party did not know if the hill had any other kind of gate, since the cloud on it did not allow an observer to see if it was barred or not.

14. Apollonius says that he went up the rock roughly from the south, following the Indian. The first thing he saw was a well four fathoms deep, from which a deep blue light rose to the surface, and whenever the sun at its zenith stood above it, this light was drawn up by the sun's ray and shot upwards looking like a rainbow of fire. He later learned that the earth at the bottom of the well was realgar, and that the Indians considered the water magical and so neither drew nor drank from it; the whole region of India round about swore by it. Near this, it seems, there was a fiery crater which gave off a lead-coloured flame; but no smoke came from it or even an odour, and the crater never overflowed, but stopped just short of spilling over its brim. There the Indians purify themselves from accidental crimes, and for that reason the Wise Men call the well 'the Well of Proof' and the fire 'the Fire of Forgiveness'. The party also says it saw two jars of black stone, the Jar of Winds and the Jar of Rains. The Jar of Rains is opened whenever India is afflicted with drought, and releases clouds, thus watering the whole land; but if there is too much rain, it is closed and so checks it. The Jar of Winds has the same effect as Aeolus's bag, I suppose, because by opening it slightly they release one of the winds to blow in due season and thus the

land prospers. They say they also saw images of gods which, if they had been Indian or Egyptian, would not have been remarkable; but in fact the oldest images in Greece, those of Athena Polias, Delian Apollo, Dionysus of Limnae, Apollo of Amyclae and other images similarly ancient have all been erected by these Indians and are worshipped with Greek ceremonies, even though they apparently live in the middle of India. They consider the peak of this hill to be the centre of the earth, and maintain a mystic flame on it which they claim to light from the sun's rays themselves; and they sing their hymn to this flame every day at noon.

15. The Wise Men's nature and their way of life on the hill are described by Apollonius himself, since in one of his addresses to the Egyptians he says, 'I saw the Indian Brahmans living on the earth and not on it, walled without walls, and with no possessions except the whole world's.' This is his rather philosophical account: Damis says that they sleep on the earth, but the earth makes a bed for them of any kind of grass they choose. He also says he saw them levitating as much as three feet from the ground, not for ostentation, since that kind of vanity is foreign to them, but because all the rites they perform to the Sun they do above the earth like him, considering this practice appropriate for the god. The fire which they draw from the sun's ray is of normal appearance, but they do not light it on an altar or keep it in a lantern; instead it is like the rays which come from the sun and are reflected by water, and apparently it is seen above the ground flickering in mid-air. They pray to the Sun on behalf of the seasons of which it is the guardian, so that they may come at the right time for the land and India may prosper; by night they pray to the sunbeam, asking it not to be at enmity with the night but remain in the form it was created by them. That is the meaning of Apollonius's saying, 'The Brahmans are on the earth and

not on the earth.' But 'walled without walls' refers to the climate in which they live, since although they appear to camp in the open air, they bring shade to cover themselves, they are not wetted when it rains, and have sunshine whenever they want.

Apollonius's saying, 'with no possessions except the whole world's' is interpreted by Damis in this way. Just as springs of water break from the earth for the worshippers of Bacchus when the god makes them and the earth quake, so they appear for the benefit of those Indians when the Indians are giving or being given a dinner. It was therefore an appropriate description of people who make no preparations in advance but obtain everything they want on the spot, when Apollonius said that they 'possess what they do not possess'.

They wear their hair long as the Spartans once did and the Thurians of Tarentum and the Melians and all the peoples that are recorded as having Spartan ways, and they tie it with a white ribbon; their feet are bare, and their style of clothing is similar to a cloak over one shoulder. The material for their clothing is wool that grows wild from the earth, white like Pamphylian wool but softer, and it exudes fat like oil. They consider this the stuff of holy garments, and if anybody except these Indians tries to pick this wool, it stays fast in the earth. The ring and the rod, both of which they carry, have a power which is capable of anything, and both are magical and highly regarded.

16. As Apollonius approached, the other Wise Men went up to him and greeted him with embraces, but Iarchas remained seated on a high chair: it was of dark copper ornamented with golden figures, while the chairs of the others were of undecorated copper and less high, since they sat at Iarchas's feet. On seeing Apollonius, Iarchas greeted him in Greek and asked for the Indian's letter. When Apollonius showed amazement at

his clairvoyance, Iarchas added that there was one letter missing in the document, a D that the writer had left out. This proved to be true; and when he had read the letter, he said, 'Apollonius, what is your opinion of us?'

'Why,' said Apollonius, 'it is shown by my taking a journey because of you which no one of the people I come from has ever taken.'

'What knowledge do you think we have that you lack?'

'It is my opinion that your ways are wiser and much more godly. But if I were to find among you nothing that I do not know, I would also have learned that there is nothing further for me to learn.'

So the Indian replied, 'Other people ask newcomers where they come from and what their mission is, but for us it is the first proof of our wisdom that we are not ignorant about our visitors. You may begin by testing this.' Whereupon he recounted Apollonius's ancestry on his father's and his mother's side, all his experiences in Aegae, how Damis joined him, all the things that they had discussed on the journey or had learned from the discussions of others. All this the Indian recited clearly and without pausing just as if he had shared the journey with them. Apollonius was amazed and asked him how he knew all this, and he replied, 'You, our visitor, have a share of this wisdom, but not yet all of it.'

'Will you let me learn it all, then?' Apollonius asked.

'Willingly,' Iarchas replied; 'that is more philosophical than grudging and concealing what is important. Besides, Apollonius, I see that you are well endowed with memory, which is the god we honour most.'

'What?' said Apollonius, 'Have you already discerned my nature?'

'Apollonius,' he replied, 'we discern every kind of soul, and have countless clues to discover them. But it is nearly noon, and we must prepare the gods' due rites; so we must attend to them, and later let us discuss whatever you like, and I invite you to attend all our ceremonies.'

'Well,' said Apollonius, 'I would certainly be doing a wrong to the Caucasus and the Indus, which I passed coming here to see you, if I did not steep myself in all your rites.'

17. 'Steep yourself,' Iarchas said, 'and let us go.' So they went to a spring of water, which Damis says he saw later and was reminded of Dirce in Boeotia. First they undressed, then they anointed their heads with an ointment like amber, which had such a warming effect on the Indians that their bodies steamed and they ran with sweat as if washing themselves with fire. Then, after diving into the water and washing, they proceeded to the temple garlanded and full of song. There they stood around in a circle and with Iarchas as their leader struck the ground with the ends of their staves; and the ground, flexing like a wave, shot them three feet into the air. They then sang a song like the Paean by Sophocles which they sing to Asclepius at Athens.[5] When they had come back to earth, Iarchas called the boy carrying the anchor and said, 'Take care of Apollonius's friends.' The boy went and returned much faster than the swiftest bird, and said, 'I have taken care of them.' Then, having carried out most of their rites, they went to rest on their chairs, and Iarchas said to the boy, 'Bring the throne of Phraotes for the wise Apollonius, so that he can sit on it for his conversation.'

18. When Apollonius had sat down, Iarchas said, 'Ask me whatever you like, since you have come among men who know everything.' So Apollonius asked if they knew themselves, expecting them to be like the Greeks in thinking it difficult to know oneself. But to Apollonius's surprise Iarchas

5. There is other evidence to connect Sophocles with the Asclepius cult at Athens.

corrected him and said, 'We know everything because we begin by knowing ourselves. None of us would approach our kind of philosophy without knowing himself first.' Apollonius remembered what he had heard from Phraotes, how the man who intends to be a philosopher tests himself before making the attempt: so he accepted this statement, having the same belief about himself. He proceeded to ask what they thought they were, and Iarchas replied, 'Gods.'

'Why?' asked Apollonius.

'Because we are good men.'

Apollonius thought that this saying showed such enlightenment that later he used it before Domitian in his speech of self-defence.

19. So he resumed the questioning, and said, 'What is your belief about the soul?'

'It is what Pythagoras taught you Greeks,' said Iarchas, 'and we taught the Egyptians.'

Apollonius replied, 'Would you say, then, that you were some Trojan or Achaean or someone before you entered this body, as Pythagoras declared himself to be Euphorbus?'

'Troy was destroyed,' said the Indian, 'by the Achaeans that sailed there then, and you Greeks have been destroyed by the tales about it. You think the only heroes are those that attacked Troy, and so you neglect a larger number of more godlike men produced by your own country, by Egypt, and by India. But since you asked me about my former body, tell me whom you think most outstanding of those that attacked or defended Troy.'

'Achilles the son of Peleus and Thetis, since Homer sings of him as a very handsome man and greater than all the other Greeks, and mentions great deeds of his. He also has a high opinion of men like Ajax and Nireus, whom he mentions as second to Achilles in beauty and nobility.'

'Compare my ancestor,' Iarchas replied, 'with Achilles, Apollonius, or rather my ancestral body, since that is what Pythagoras considered Euphorbus. [20.] You see, there was a time when the Ethiopians lived here and were an Indian tribe. As yet Ethiopia did not exist, but Egypt had its boundary at Meroe and the Cataracts, and the same country contained the source of the Nile and ended at its mouth. As long as the Ethiopians lived here as subjects of King Ganges, the earth fed them plentifully and the gods protected them. But they killed their king, and were considered unclean by the other Indians. The earth, too, no longer let them stay; it destroyed the seed that they put in it before it came to the sheath, it aborted women's conception, and gave poor fodder to the cattle, and wherever they founded a city, the earth caved in and gave way beneath. Moreover, the ghost of Ganges drove them on as they progressed, causing terror among the mob, and gave them no peace until they had sacrificed to the earth the murderers and those that had stained their hands with blood. This Ganges was fifteen feet tall, beautiful as no other man ever was, and was the son of the river Ganges. His father had flooded India, but he diverted it into the Red Sea[6] and reconciled it with the land: for this reason the earth produced plenty for him while he lived, and took vengeance when he died. Now Homer makes Achilles come to Troy for Helen, and says that he had captured twelve cities by sea and eleven by land, and that he flew into a fury when the king took a woman away from him, showing himself harsh and savage. Let us compare the Indian with this. He founded sixty cities, the most esteemed in the country; and there is nobody who thinks sacking cities is more glorious than building them. He also repulsed the Scythians from above the Caucasus when they

6. In antiquity the Red Sea denoted the Indian Ocean and its off-shoots, the Persian Gulf, Gulfs of Aqaba and Suez, and our Red Sea. 'Red Sea' can refer to any of these bodies of water.

made an attack once on this land; and to prove your courage defending the liberty of your own land is far better than bringing slavery on a city, especially when it is because of a woman who probably did not mind being carried off. He made an alliance with the ruler of the land that Phraotes now rules; and when the man, in sheer lawlessness and lust, took away his wife, he did not break his treaty, saying he had sworn so solemnly that he could not harm him even when wronged.

21. 'I could tell you more about him, except that I am reluctant to start praising myself, since, you see, I am that man. I proved this when I was four. This Ganges once drove seven swords of adamant into the earth so that no danger could come near this land, and the gods ordered us to go where the swords were planted and sacrifice, but they did not reveal the place where they were. Still just a child, I led the prophets to a ditch and told them to dig, saying that the swords were deposited there. You must not be surprised at me for passing from one Indian to another. He' (pointing to a youth about twenty years old) 'is better fitted to study philosophy than any man, and his body is strong, as you see, and excellently endowed, so as to be indifferent to fire and any surgery. Yet with these gifts he is an enemy of philosophy.'

'What is wrong with the boy, Iarchas?' asked Apollonius. 'It is a shame if he does not embrace philosophy when he is so prepared for it by nature, and if he does not love learning even though he associates with you.'

'He doesn't associate with us,' replied Iarchas. 'He is like a lion, captive against his will, a prisoner who suspects us when we tame him and pet him. This boy was once Palamedes at Troy, and his two greatest enemies are Odysseus and Homer, Odysseus because he devised a scheme against him which caused him to be stoned, Homer because he did not think him worth so much as a line. Since the wisdom he had did him no good, and he got no praise from Homer, who brought fame to many men of no importance at all, and became the victim of Odysseus when he had done him no wrong, he is an enemy of philosophy and feels aggrieved at what was done to him. This, then, is Palamedes, and he can write without having learned to do so.'

. . . . .

38. In the middle of this conversation, the Wise Men were interrupted by the messenger bringing some Indians who needed cures. For instance, he brought forward a woman praying to them on her son's behalf. He was sixteen years old, she said, but had been possessed for two years by a spirit with a sly, deceitful character. One of the wise men asked what her evidence was, and she said, 'This boy of mine is rather hand-some in appearance, and the spirit is in love with him. He will not allow him to be rational, or go to school or to archery-training, or to stay at home either, but carries him off into deserted places. My boy no longer has his natural voice but speaks in deep, ringing tones like a man; his eyes, too, are more someone else's than his own. All this makes me weep and tear my hair, and I scold my son as you would expect, but he does not recognize me. But when I decided on this journey, which I did a year ago, the spirit confessed who he was, using my son as a medium. He said he was the ghost of a man who formerly died in war, still very much in love with his wife; but the woman broke their marriage bond three days after his death by marrying another man, and from that time, he said, he had loathed the love of women and had transferred his affection to my son. And he promised that if I did not accuse him before you he would give many wonderful presents to the boy; and this rather made me change my mind. But he has been keeping me waiting for a long time now, acting

as sole master of my house, with his wicked, deceitful ways.'[7]

The Wise Man then asked her if the boy was with her, but she said, 'No: I did everything to make him come, but that spirit threatened me with mention of "cliffs" and "abysses", saying he would kill my son if I accused him here.'

'Don't worry,' said the Wise Man; 'he will not kill him when he has read this,' and he brought a letter out of his pocket and gave it to the woman; it was addressed to the spirit, and contained threats and warnings.

39. Besides that, there came a man of about thirty, who was lame; he had been an expert lion-hunter but had been attacked by a lion and had dislocated his hip, and so was lame in one leg. But the Wise Man massaged his hip and thus restored the man to an upright walk. Someone else who had gone blind went away with his sight fully restored, and another man with a paralysed arm left strong again. A woman, too, who had had seven miscarriages was cured through the prayers of her husband as follows. The Wise Man told the husband, when his wife was in labour, to bring a live hare under his cloak to the place where she was, walk around her, and immediately release the hare: for she would lose her womb as well as the foetus if the hare was not immediately driven out.

. . . . .

50. So much for the conversations between Apollonius and the Wise Men. He had stayed there for four months and absorbed all their doctrines, both avowed and secret. When he decided to leave, they persuaded him to send the guide and the camels to Phraotes with a letter, while they themselves

7. A similar homosexual infatuation of an invisible demon with a boy is unforgettably depicted in Goethe's poem, *Erlkönig* (which Franz Schubert set to music).

gave him another guide and camels, and sent him on his way, congratulating themselves as well as him. They embraced Apollonius, saying that ordinary people would regard him as a god, in life as well as in death; and then they went back to their place of meditation, though looking back at him and showing their unwillingness to let him go. Apollonius kept the Ganges on his right and Hyphasis on his left, and after ten days' journey from the sacred hill reached the sea. As they travelled, they saw many ostriches, wild oxen, asses, lions, leopards, tigers, and a kind of monkey different from the ones in the pepper groves, black and hairy, with a similarity to dogs and the size of small men. As they talked about the sights in their usual way, they reached the sea, and there they found small trading-stations had been set up, with ferry-boats like the ones in Etruria moored there. The Red Sea is apparently very blue, and is named, as I mentioned, after Erythras, who gave his name to that stretch of sea.[8]

51. When Apollonius had arrived there, he sent the camel back to Iarchas with this letter.

'Apollonius greets Iarchas and the other Wise Men.

'I came to you by land, and you have shown me the sea; but you also shared your native wisdom with me, and showed me a path through heaven. I will recall all this to the Greeks, and enjoy your conversations as if you were present, unless I have had only a useless, tantalizing taste of them. Good-bye, good philosophers.'

52. So he boarded a ship, and sailed on a gentle, favouring breeze, wondering at the estuary of the Hyphasis and how dangerous it is where it meets the sea: as I mentioned, it finally runs into rocky, narrow places and over precipices, and

8. *Erythros* is Greek for 'red', hence Philostratus's etymology. See the note on III. 20 above for what was meant by 'Red Sea' in antiquity.

after these it pours into the sea through one mouth, proving dangerous to sailors who cling too close to shore.

53. They claim also to have seen the mouth of the Indus, with a city called Patala built there surrounded by the river. It was here that Alexander's fleet came, under the captaincy of Nearchus, who was very experienced in commands at sea. Damis agrees with everything that Orthagoras says about the Red Sea, that the Pole Star is not visible from it, sailors cannot tell the south, and the visible stars leave their natural positions; we must therefore believe that these accounts are correct with respect to the sky in these parts. They also mention a little island called Biblus where the mussels, oysters, and other such things growing on the rocks are ten times the size of Greek ones. The pearls that are taken there have white shells, and take the place of the oyster's heart.

54. They also seem to have put in at Pagadae in the land of the Oreitae. In this land the rocks are of copper, the sand is of copper, and rivers bring down copper dust: but the natives consider that the earth produces gold because of the purity of the copper.

55. They say they also came across the Fish-Eaters, whose city is Stobera. These apparently wear the skins of very large fish; the sheep there smell of fish and have a strange diet – the shepherds feed them on fish, as they feed sheep on figs in Caria. The Carmanian Indians are a friendly tribe, and the sea they live on is so full of fish that they do not even store them, or salt them as they do on the Pontus; they sell a few, and put most of them back into the sea still gasping.

56. It seems that they also put in at Balara, which is a port full of myrtle- and palm-trees; they saw laurels there too, and the

place has an abundance of springs. It is full of every kind of vegetable- and flower-garden, and the harbours there are extremely calm. Opposite this region, separated by a strait of twelve and a half miles, lies a sacred island called Selera, inhabited by a mermaid who is a fearful being: she carries off many who sail there, and makes it impossible for a ship even to throw a cable to the island.

57. It would not be right to omit the description of another kind of pearl, since Apollonius did not find the story puerile either; it is very interesting and as amazing as any wonder of the sea. Where the island faces the open sea, the water is of unfathomable depth, and produces a white-shelled oyster which is full of liquid but produces no stone at all. The natives wait for a calm, and in fact themselves make the sea settle by pouring olive oil on it, which has this effect. A diver goes down to find the oyster, equipped in every respect like a sponge-gatherer except that he has an iron block and a phial of perfume. The Indian then sits beside the oyster and tempts it with the perfume until it opens and gets intoxicated with it; then he opens it with a needle and makes it squirt its juice, which he catches in the block. This is a perforated mould, and the juice immediately turns to stone and becomes solid, like natural pearls, so that the pearl is the white blood of the Red Sea. They say that the Arabians who live opposite also go in for this kind of fishing. Thereafter the sea is apparently all full of animals, and whales swim through it in herds. To keep them away, the ships carry bells fore and aft, and the sound frightens the creatures, and so stops them from approaching the ships.

58. They sailed into the estuary of the Euphrates and sailed up it to Babylon to visit Vardanes, whom they found just as they remembered him before. They then went back to Nineveh;

and since Antioch had its usual rowdiness, with no interest in Greek culture, they went down to the sea at Seleuceia. There they met a ship and sailed to Cyprus, putting in at Paphos where the idol of Aphrodite is.[9] Apollonius admired its symbolic shape, and gave the priests considerable guidance about the rites of the temple. Thence he sailed to Ionia, winning great admiration and high esteem from all friends of wisdom.

9. The idol was non-representational, shaped like a cone. Tacitus describes it in his *Histories* II. 3.

BOOK IV

4. A plague was approaching Ephesus, and before the disease broke out, Apollonius was aware of its imminence, and foretold it accordingly. Often in his discourses he would say, 'Earth, stay as you are' and, in threatening tones, such things as 'Save these people' and 'You are not to come here.' But the inhabitants paid no notice, and were all the more inclined to think such things exaggeration because Apollonius visited all the sanctuaries and so appeared to be averting and exorcising the plague. Since they were indifferent to their fate, he decided that he should not help them any longer, and travelled around the rest of Ionia, improving the customs in each place and always discoursing to his audiences on subjects beneficial to them.

5. When he approached Smyrna, the Ionians came out to meet him, since they were making the Panionian sacrifice at the time.[1] He also received a decree of the Ionians in which they asked him to join their festival. In this Apollonius came across a name which was not Ionic at all, since appended to the motion was the name 'Lucullus'. So he sent a letter to their Assembly criticizing them for their barbarism: he also found a 'Fabricius' and other such people named in the resolution.[2] His letter on the subject shows how severely he reproached them.

1. A reference to a festival of all the Ionian cities in honour of Poseidon.
2. Easterners who had acquired Roman citizenship were entitled to take on Roman names, which were frequently combined with one of their Greek names. By way of affectation, non-citizens sometimes used Roman names, to which they were not entitled; and often, in local affairs, those who *were* entitled to use them did not. Apollonius deplores the ostentatious use of Roman names.

6. On another day he came before the Ionians and said, 'What is this bowl?'

'The Panionian bowl,' they replied.

He then drew from it, poured a libation, and said, 'You gods that guide Ionia, let this beautiful colony enjoy safety from the sea. Let no disaster burst from the sea on to the land. Do not let Aegaeon the Earth-Shaker ever shatter the cities.' This was what he pronounced, foreseeing, I suppose, what later happened to Smyrna, Miletus, Chios, Samos, and many of the Ionian cities.[3]

7. He saw that the Smyrnaeans followed every kind of knowledge eagerly, and so he encouraged them and gave them more eagerness. They must put more pride in themselves, he told them, than in the appearance of their city; even if it was the most beautiful on earth, with the sea at its disposal and always supplied with a west wind, still its sons were a finer adornment than colonnades, pictures and excess of gold. Buildings stayed in one place, never seen anywhere except in their own part of the world, while good men were seen and spoken of everywhere, and they made the city of their origin great in proportion to the number of them that could travel the world. Cities as beautiful as Smyrna, he said, were like the statue of Zeus made by Phidias at Olympia. It was seated, since that was the decision of the artist, whereas good men went everywhere, and were no different from Homer's Zeus, whom the poet describes in many shapes, and who is a more marvellous creation than the Zeus of ivory; for this Zeus was

3. Perhaps an allusion to the great earthquake of A.D. 16, but if so, anachronistically. Earthquakes were not uncommon in Asia Minor, and this passage may refer to one otherwise unknown. Some have conjectured that the reference is to one or another of the great earthquakes of the Antonine Age in the second century A.D.

visible on earth, while the other was supposed to be in every-thing in the universe.

8. Moreover, he gave the Smyrnaeans a disquisition on security in the conduct of cities, because he saw that they were quarrelling with one another and had no agreed policy. He told them that to behave rightly a city needed unity with faction. This seemed implausible and confusing, so that Apollonius, aware that most of them could not follow his meaning, said, 'Black and white can never be the same, and sweet and bitter can never mix properly, but unity joined with faction will keep a city from harm. You must understand what I mean in this way. The kind of faction that induces sword-fights and stoning should be avoided by a city, since what it needs is child-welfare, law, and citizens to whom speech and action can be entrusted. But there is a kind of mutual competition for the common good, in which one man seeks to give better advice than another, or to hold office better than another, or go on an embassy, or erect finer buildings than when another man was commissioner: and this, I think, is beneficial strife, faction between citizens for the public good. The idea that every man should have different pursuits and contribute them to the public benefit was long ago considered foolish by the Spartans: they practised the arts of war, and war was their whole passion and their only interest. But in my opinion it is best that everybody does what he knows and what he can. If one man has a high reputation for persuasiveness, another for wisdom, another for using his wealth for the public good, another for his virtue, another for his implacable severity towards wrong-doing, another for his incorruptibility, the city will be firmly grounded, or rather exalted.'[4]

4. This discourse is a brief but characteristic representative of the many discourses delivered by philosophers and sophists on the subject of faction and concord in cities. We possess good specimens by Dio Chrysostom and Aelius Aristides.

9. Just as he was making this speech he saw a three-masted ship sailing out of harbour with each of the sailors doing different things to prepare the voyage. He called his audience's attention to it and said, 'Do you see the crew of that ship? The rowers have manned the boats, others are raising and weighing anchors, some are spreading the sails to the wind, others looking out from the prow and the stern. If one of them omits one of these jobs or goes about his profession inexpertly, they will have a bad voyage and prove to be their own storm. But if they compete with one another, and turn their faction to proving themselves as good as the next man, this ship will have safe harbour, all will be calm sea and prosperous voyage, and the foresight they show will prove to be Poseidon the Bringer of Safety.'

10. With speeches like this he brought calm to Smyrna. In Ephesus, however, the plague had arrived and nothing proved effective against it. They sent an embassy to Apollonius, therefore, hoping to make him the curer of their misfortune. He decided to make the journey without delay, and after merely saying, 'Let us go', he was in Ephesus, imitating, I suppose, Pythagoras's famous miracle of being in Thurii and Metapontum both at once. He summoned the Ephesians together, and said, 'Don't worry. I will end the plague today.'

So saying, he led them all, young and old, towards the theatre where the statue of the Averter stands.[5] There they found what appeared to be an old beggar, pretending to have his eyes closed. He carried a bag and a lump of bread in it, and had ragged clothing and a wrinkled face. Apollonius made the Ephesians stand around the man, and said, 'Collect as many

5. The statue of the Averter took the shape of Hercules, as we learn from the end of this chapter. It was clearly as a result of this incident that the Ephesians later revered Apollonius as Hercules *Alexikakos*, 'Averter of Evil' (Lactantius, *div. inst.* V. 3).

stones as possible and throw them at this outcast.' The Ephesians were puzzled by his meaning and shocked at the thought
of killing someone who was a visitor and so destitute, and the
man also pleaded with them, saying everything to gain their
pity. But Apollonius urged the Ephesians relentlessly to crush
the man and not let him escape. When some of them hit him
from a distance and the man, who had appeared to have his
eyes closed, suddenly opened them and showed them to be full
of fire, the Ephesians realized it was a spirit and threw so many
stones that a pile of them built up over him. After a while
Apollonius told them to remove the stones and to discover the
beast that they had killed. When they uncovered the man they
thought they had stoned, he had vanished; instead they saw a
dog resembling a Molossian hound but the size of the largest
lion, crushed by the stones and spewing foam like a dog with
rabies. The statue of the Averter, in the shape of Hercules,
stands near the spot where the apparition was stoned.

· · · · ·

19. Damis says that Apollonius gave very many lectures at
Athens, but that he had recorded only those of them that were
essential and addressed to important subjects. Because Apollonius saw that the Athenians were fond of making sacrifices,
he gave his first discourse on religion, and how to make the
right sacrifice, libation, or prayer to each god, and at which
time of night or day. One may also come across a book of
Apollonius in which he gives these instructions in his own
words.[6] He gave this lesson at Athens primarily as a tribute to
his wisdom and theirs, but also to show up the hierophant for
his blasphemous and ignorant talk,[7] since nobody thereafter

6. A reference to Apollonius's book on sacrifices, mentioned previously in this work by Philostratus at III. 41 (omitted in this translation).

7. In the chapter immediately preceding, omitted here, a priest
(hierophant) of the Eleusinian Mysteries called Apollonius a charlatan.
Apollonius foretold the priest's successor.

could think that a man who lectured on the right way to cultivate the gods was impure in religious matters.

. . . . .

25. At that time, Demetrius was lecturing in Corinth, a man who had all the strength of Cynic philosophy: Favorinus later mentioned him quite frequently in many of his discourses.[8] Apollonius had the same effect on him as the wisdom of Socrates is said to have had on Antisthenes: he followed him, eager to learn and devoted to his lectures, and tried to send his own pupils to Apollonius.

One of these was Menippus of Lycia, twenty-five years old, very intelligent and physically well endowed, since in appearance he resembled a handsome and well-bred athlete. It was generally believed that Menippus was the lover of a foreign woman. This woman appeared to be beautiful and very extravagant, and claimed to be rich, but in fact she was none of these things at all – it was all a delusion. Menippus had been walking alone along the road to Cenchreae when a spirit in the form of a woman met him, grasped his hand, and said she had been in love with him for a long time; she was Phoenician, and lived in a suburb of Corinth. Naming one of the suburbs, she said, 'Come there this evening, and you will have a song sung by me, and wine such as you have never tasted. There will be no rival in your way, but we will share our beauty between ourselves.' The youth was seduced by this, since despite his proficiency in other parts of philosophy, he was a slave to love-affairs. He went to her house in the evening, and visited her often thereafter as if she was his catamite, not yet realizing she was a spirit.

Apollonius looked at Menippus like a sculptor, getting an

8. Favorinus wàs a second-century hermaphrodite philosopher and rhetor from Arles. Philostratus later included a concise biography of him in his *Lives of the Sophists*.

impression and a view of him. Then, sizing him up, he said, 'Ah, you are the beautiful boy that beautiful women chase. You are cuddling a snake, and a snake is cuddling you.'

Menippus was bewildered, and Apollonius said, 'You have a woman who is not your wife. Well, do you think she is in love with you?'

'Certainly,' was the reply, 'since she treats me as a woman in love would.'

'Would you marry her?'

'Yes, it would be a joy to marry a woman that loved you.'

So Apollonius asked, 'When is the wedding?'

'It's imminent,' the boy replied, 'tomorrow perhaps.'

So Apollonius waited for the time of the wedding-feast, and interrupted the guests when they had just arrived. 'Where is the extravagant lady in whose honour you have come?' he asked.

'Here,' said Menippus, at the same time rising with a blush.

'And the silver, the gold, and the other decorations of the banqueting-hall – which of you owns them?'

'My wife,' he replied; 'all I have is this,' pointing to his philosopher's cloak.

'Do you all know,' asked Apollonius, 'about Tantalus's gardens, which both exist and do not exist?'[9]

'Yes,' they said, 'from Homer, since we have not been down to Hades.'

'Let me tell you,' said Apollonius, 'that that is what these decorations are; they are the insubstantial appearance of substance. To show you what I mean, this excellent bride is a vampire, though most people think vampires are the same as sirens and werewolves. Vampires also love sex, but above all they love human flesh and use sex as a trap for those they want to eat.'

The woman said, 'Be quiet, and go away,' pretending to

9. cf. *Odyssey* XI. 585.

95

find his conversation disgusting, and also making fun of philosophers for always talking nonsense. But then the golden cups and the illusory silver proved insubstantial, and all faded from sight, and the cup-bearers, cooks and the other servants vanished under Apollonius's scrutiny. Whereupon the creature pretended to weep, begging him not to interrogate it or force it to confess its true nature. But Apollonius insisted relentlessly, until it confessed it was a vampire, fattening Menippus with pleasures in order to eat his body, since it was its custom to devour beautiful young bodies because their blood was fresh.

This is the most famous of the stories about Apollonius.[10] However, I have been obliged to tell it in full, because although most people know of it as something that happened in the middle of Greece, they have only heard the gist of it, that Apollonius once unmasked a siren in Corinth; they as yet do not know how it acted and that Apollonius saved Menippus. Damis, however, has told the tale, and so have I from his account.

. . . . . .

33. Another incident in Sparta was a letter from the emperor to the Lacedaemonians, criticizing their state for using more licence than their freedom allowed; and it was because of the slanders of the governor of Greece that this letter had been sent to them.[11] The Spartans were in a quandary, and their city was at variance with itself as to whether they should write

10. This story was told by Robert Burton in his *Anatomy of Melancholy* and was the inspiration of Keats's poem *Lamia* (cf. Introduction, p. 21 above). The story also calls to mind Goethe's vampire poem, *Die Braut von Korinth*.

11. The trouble mentioned here is presumably connected with the political disputes of two brothers, descended from the Spartan dynast Eurycles. One of them, C. Julius Spartiaticus, was exiled in the latter part of Nero's reign.

placating the emperor's anger or despising it. They therefore called in Apollonius to advise them on the nature of the letter, and when he saw their division, he came into their assembly and made this brief speech: 'Palamedes discovered writing, not only so that we should write, but also so that we should know what not to write.' In this way he diverted the Spartans from appearing either rash or cowardly.

. . . . .

35. Nero did not tolerate philosophy. Its practitioners he considered inquisitive creatures who concealed a power of divination, and the philosopher's cloak was once used in evidence as the proof of a diviner. To mention only one, Musonius of Babylon,[12] a man second only to Apollonius, was put into chains because of his wisdom and during his confinement was in danger of his life. In fact he would have died for all his oppressor cared, if he had not had a very strong constitution.

36. This was the situation of philosophy at the time when Apollonius was nearing Rome. When he was fifteen miles away from it, he met Philolaus of Citium near the grove of Aricia. Philolaus, a practised speaker but too cowardly to endure any danger, was on his way from Rome. He looked like a man running away, and urged every philosopher he met to do the same. Addressing Apollonius, he advised him to yield to circumstances and not visit Rome when philosophy was out of favour; and as he described what was happening there, he kept turning around in case someone was listening behind him.

12. The reference is to the philosopher Musonius Rufus, an Etruscan. It makes no sense to say 'of Babylon'; a corruption in the text may be suspected. Further on, in VII. 16, Philostratus rightly calls Musonius an Etruscan.

'You,' he said, 'are coming with a whole circle of philosophers attached to you, and are sure to be disliked. Don't you know about the men that Nero has posted at the gates? They will arrest you and your friends before you get inside.'

'What are the emperor's interests said to be, Philolaus?' asked Apollonius.

'He races in public,' was the reply, 'he goes on the Roman stage and sings, he lives with gladiators, and is a gladiator and a killer himself.'[13]

'Well, my friend,' replied Apollonius, 'what more profitable spectacle do you think educated men could have than an emperor who disgraces himself? Man is the plaything of god, as Plato taught us, but an emperor who becomes the plaything of man, and degrades himself to please the masses, could be a source of endless reflections for lovers of wisdom.'

'Certainly,' said Philolaus, 'if it could be done without danger: but suppose you die under arrest, and Nero eats you alive before you have seen any of his acts? That will be a high price for meeting him, a higher price than Odysseus paid when he visited the Cyclops and lost many of his comrades because he felt an urge to see him and could not resist the monstrous, cruel spectacle.'

Apollonius however said, 'Do you think that this man is less blind than the Cyclops, if he does such things?'

Philolaus replied, 'He can do what he likes, but you should at least keep these men safe.'

37. These words he said in a louder voice, appearing to shed tears. This made Damis worry in case the young men might be weakened by Philolaus's timorousness, and so he took Apollonius aside and said, 'This hare will ruin the young men, infecting them all with his terror and despondency.'

13. This was true of Nero (except, possibly, living with gladiators).

Apollonius replied, 'There are many blessings that the gods have sent me often without my even asking, but I would say that the greatest benefit is the present one. A test has come my way which will distinguish for sure which of the young men are philosophers and which of them have a completely different interest.' Immediately those of them who lacked strength were shown up; dismayed by Philolaus's conversation, some pleaded illness, others lack of provisions, others homesickness, others terrifying dreams, until Apollonius was reduced from thirty-four disciples to eight, who went with him to Rome, while the others ran as fast as they could away from Nero and philosophy.

38. Apollonius assembled those that remained, who included Menippus who had had the affair with the vampire, Dioscorides of Egypt, and Damis; and he said, 'I will not reproach those who deserted you, but praise you for proving to be men of my own kind. And I will not think a man a coward for leaving in fear of Nero, but rather give the title of philosopher to anyone who turns out to be above such fears, and I will teach them all I know.

'First, I think that we should thank the gods for putting these decisions into your minds and the others'. Next, we should make the gods our guides, since without them we have no other helper. We must approach the city that rules so many parts of the earth; and how could one enter it without the gods' guidance? All the more so since it has so oppressive a tyranny established inside it that wisdom is forbidden. Nobody ought to think it folly to be cheerful about a journey that many philosophers are avoiding: for one thing, I do not think that anything on earth could prove so terrifying as ever to dismay a wise man, and besides I would not set up a test of courage that did not involve danger.

'Furthermore, I have covered more land than any man ever

did, seeing a multitude of beasts in Arabia and India, but I have no idea how many heads this beast has, this beast generally called a tyrant, or whether it has crooked talons and jagged teeth. This beast is said to be a city-creature and to live in the middle of cities, but its nature is more wild than the mountain or forest variety; lions and leopards are sometimes soothed and tamed into changing their ways, whereas this creature is incited by stroking to become even more savage than it is naturally, and to devour everything. You could never say of animals that they devoured their mothers, whereas Nero has gorged himself on that kind of flesh. It is true the same happened to Orestes and Alcmaeon, but they have an excuse for what they did; the father of the one was killed by his own wife, and the father of the other was bartered for a trinket. This man, on the contrary, was adopted by an aged emperor through his mother's efforts, and inherited the power, and yet he killed his mother by devising a ship for her that killed her offshore.[14]

'All this may make some people think Nero terrifying, and that may scare them from philosophy because they think it unsafe to practise something that displeases him. But they should recall that the balance of terror lies with those who follow moderation and wisdom, since such men are on good terms with the gods. They should also consider the behaviour of the lawless as petty rather than terrifying, since drunkards too we consider silly rather than terrifying. So let us proceed to Rome, if we have the strength; and we can use against the pronouncements of Nero banishing philosophy the line of Sophocles, "Indeed it was not Zeus that gave this order,"[15] or the Muses or Apollo the Prophet. I expect Nero too knows this verse, being fond of tragedy, I believe.'

14. False: Nero's mother, Agrippina, escaped from the lethal ship and had to be put to death on land (Tacitus, *Annals* XIV. 3–8).

15. *Antigone*, 450.

At that moment one might recall Homer's lines to the effect that when a speech unites warlike men, they become 'one helmet and one shield,'[16] and might find the same thing happening with these men. They were cemented together by Apollonius's words so that they had the strength to die for philosophy and to show that they had more courage than those that had run away.

39. When they approached the gates, the guards asked them no question, but simply stared at their clothes in amazement, because their appearance seemed holy and not at all like that of beggars. They had put up at an inn near the gates and were having dinner, since it was by now evening, when a man came in drunk, as if he were merrymaking. He had quite a pleasant voice, and used to go around Rome singing Nero's songs for pay: if anybody listened without interest or did not pay for the performance, the man was privileged to arrest him for treason. He also had a lyre and all the equipment appropriate for playing it, and he kept stored in a box a lyre string which had already been used and strung. He claimed it was from Nero's lyre, and that he had bought it for two minae and would not sell it to anybody unless they were lyre players of the first rank and competitors at the Pythian games. So he struck up in his usual way, and after completing a short hymn started on songs by Nero, some from the *Oresteia*, some from the *Antigone*, and similarly from other plays in which the emperor had performed; and the man played all the tortuous melodies that Nero warbled in his ugly coloratura. When the party proved rather uninterested in his song, he claimed that they were disrespecting Nero and were enemies of the Divine Voice, but they paid no attention. Menippus asked Apollonius how he could listen to the man talking in this way, and Apollonius replied, 'Just as I listened to him singing. But do not let us be

16. *Iliad* XIII. 131.

annoyed by this; let us pay him for his exhibition and enable him to sacrifice to Nero's Muses.'

40. That was the end of that insult. Early the next day Telesinus, one of the two consuls,[17] summoned Apollonius and said, 'What are these clothes?'

'Pure,' Apollonius replied, 'and made of nothing perishable.'

'What kind of philosophy do you practise?'

'Religion, and the way to pray and sacrifice to the gods.'

'My good philosopher, doesn't everybody know that?'

'Many do not; and anybody that does have a proper understanding of these things might be greatly improved if he were told by a wiser man that what he knows is correct.'

Telesinus was rather given to religious observances, and when he heard this, he recognized Apollonius from what he had long since been told about him. He thought he ought not to ask his name openly in case Apollonius wished somebody not to know it yet: so he brought him back to the subject of the gods, as he was fond of discussions; and treating Apollonius as a wise man, he said, 'What prayer do you make when you approach the altars?'

'I pray that justice may exist, that the laws be not broken, that wise men be poor and others be rich, but without crime.'

'Do you think you will be granted so many prayers, then?' asked Telesinus.

'Of course,' replied Apollonius, 'because I include them all in one prayer, asking for this when I approach the altars: "Gods, give me my due." If I am a good man, I will get more than what I mentioned, but if the gods count me among the wicked, I will get the opposite from them. I will not

17. C. Luccius Telesinus was consul with C. Suetonius Paulinus in A.D. 66.

blame them, if I am thought to deserve evil, not being good myself.'

Telesinus was struck by this speech, and to do Apollonius a favour said, 'You may visit any shrine. I will write to the priests telling them to welcome you and to adopt your improvements.'

'If you don't write,' said Apollonius, 'will they not welcome me?'

'No,' he replied, 'that is in my power.'

'I am glad,' said Apollonius, 'that an important power is in the hands of a good man, but there is something else about me I would like you to know. I like to live in any sanctuary that is not completely closed; none of the gods refuses me, but they let me share their roof. Please grant me this, just as the barbarians allowed me.'

Telesinus replied, 'The barbarians have anticipated the Romans in a very praiseworthy deed. I would like the same to be said of me.'

Apollonius therefore lived in the sanctuaries, moving and changing from one to another. When criticized for this, he said, 'Even the gods do not live in heaven all the time. They travel to Ethiopia, to Olympia and to Athos. I think it illogical that the gods travel around every country of mankind, while men do not visit all the gods. Moreover, masters who pay no attention to their servants are not blamed, since perhaps they neglect them for being no good; but servants that did not show all due respect to their masters would be killed by them for being abominable and "damned slaves".'

41. When he discoursed on sacred subjects, the gods were worshipped more, and people came to him thinking that their blessings from the gods would be increased. Associating with him was not yet frowned upon, because he conversed

publicly and talked to everybody. He did not hang about other men's doors, or spend time with the powerful, but greeted them if they visited him, and had the same discussions with them as with the common people.

42. Then, however, Demetrius arrived in Rome after Apollonius, having the same friendly attitude towards him that I mentioned in the part of my work that dealt with Corinth.[18] But while he honoured Apollonius, he attacked Nero, and so this became suspected as a plot of Apollonius, who was thought to be inciting Demetrius personally to this course. This was all the more true when Nero completed a gymnasium that was the most amazing in Rome.[19] Nero himself with the Great Council and the knights of Rome was celebrating a holiday in it, when Demetrius came right in and gave a denunciation of people who bathed, saying that they were weakening and defiling themselves, and he claimed that such things were a useless extravagance. The only thing that saved him from being executed on the spot was the fact that Nero was in his best singing voice that day; he sang in a tavern built to supply the gymnasium, while he stood, like the most shameless tradesman, naked except at the waist. Even so Demetrius did not escape danger because of what he had said, since Tigellinus, who had the command of Nero's sword,[20] expelled him from Rome for ruining the bathhouse with his speech. Tigellinus also secretly set a watch on Apollonius for when he too would say something punishable and unguarded.

43. But Apollonius showed neither open indifference nor the concern that people have when guarding against danger. He

18. Above, Book IV. 25.

19. Built in A.D. 60–62.

20. Ofonius Tigellinus became prefect of the praetorian guard after the death of Sextus Afranius Burrus in A.D. 62.

simply discussed the subject at hand in the company of Telesinus and other men who thought that even if philosophy was in a dangerous position, they would not run any risk conversing with Apollonius. But he was suspected, as I have mentioned, and all the more so for what he said about an omen. There was an eclipse of the sun accompanied by thunder, which is considered very unusual in an eclipse. Apollonius looked up at the sky and said, 'Something momentous is going to happen and not happen.' Those present at his discourse could not as yet interpret his statement. Three days later, however, they all understood his meaning: Nero was at dinner and a thunderbolt hit the table, breaking a cup when it was in his hands and not far from his lips. Apollonius had referred to his coming so close to being struck as something that was going to happen and not happen. When Tigellinus heard this story, he was afraid of Apollonius as one who must have supernatural knowledge. He decided, therefore, not to bring open charges against him in case Apollonius did him some invisible harm. But he scrutinized Apollonius's conversation, his silence, when he sat down, when he walked, whatever he ate and with whom, and whether he sacrificed or not, using for the purpose all the eyes that the prefect's office has to see with.

44. Rome had an epidemic of the illness called by doctors catarrh; it causes coughing and has a bad effect on the voices of people talking. The temples were full of people praying to the gods, since Nero's throat was swollen and his voice was hoarse. Apollonius felt indignant at the general madness, but criticized nobody: in fact when Menippus expressed outrage at these events, Apollonius restrained him and checked him with the advice to pardon the gods for enjoying the capers of buffoons.

This remark came to Tigellinus's ears, and he sent agents to take Apollonius to prison before answering a charge of treason against Nero. An accuser was primed against Apollonius, a man who had already caused the deaths of many and had a string of such triumphs. This man had a paper in his hands with the charge written on it, and he waved it at Apollonius like a sword, saying that it had been sharpened and would finish him off. But when Tigellinus unrolled the paper, he found no trace of writing on it, but instead saw a blank sheet. This made him suspect something supernatural, the same effect as Apollonius is later said to have had on Domitian; and so Tigellinus took him off to his secret court, where the holders of this office sit privately on affairs of the greatest moment. Dismissing everyone, he plied Apollonius with questions about himself. Apollonius named his father, his city, and the object for which he studied wisdom; this, he claimed, was to know the gods and to understand men, since knowing oneself was less difficult than knowing another.

'How do you unmask spirits and ghostly apparitions, Apollonius?' asked Tigellinus.

'The way I unmask murderous and impious humans,' he replied with a sneer at Tigellinus, who was the man who had taught Nero all his cruelty and profligacy.

'Would you give me a prophecy,' he asked, 'if I requested one?'

'How can I?' replied Apollonius; 'I am no prophet.'

'Yet they say you are the man who said something momentous was going to happen and not happen.'

'What you have heard is true, but don't ascribe it to the gift of prophecy rather than to knowledge which god reveals to wise men.'

'Why is it that you do not fear Nero?'

'Because god, who made him seem terrifying, has granted me the gift of not feeling terror.'

'What is your opinion of Nero?'

'Better than yours. You all think singing suits him, but I think silence does.'

Tigellinus was overcome, and said, 'Provide sureties for your person, and go.'

'Who will give sureties,' asked Apollonius, 'for a person that no one can imprison?'

Tigellinus decided that these words were supernatural and beyond human ken, and to avoid fighting with the gods he said, 'Go where you like. You are too powerful to be governed by me.'

45. Apollonius performed another miracle. There was a girl who appeared to have died just at the time of her wedding. The groom followed the bier, with all the lamentations of an unconsummated marriage, and the city of Rome mourned with him, since the girl was from a family of consular rank.[21] Apollonius appeared on the scene and said, 'Put the bier down. I will stop you crying for the girl.' Immediately he asked her name, which made most people think he was going to declaim a speech of the kind delivered at funerals to raise lamentation. But Apollonius merely touched her and said something secretly over her, waking the girl up from her apparent death. Immediately the girl spoke, and went back to her father's house like Alcestis brought back to life by Hercules. Her kinsmen gave Apollonius a hundred and fifty thousand drachmas, but he said he was giving it as an extra dowry for the girl. He may have seen a spark of life in her which her doctors had not noticed, since apparently it was drizzling and steam was coming from her face; or he may have revived and restored her life when it was extinguished; but the true explanation of this has proved unfathomable, to me no less than to the bystanders.

21. Her immediate family included a consul. cf. this story with Luke VII. 12–15.

46. It was at that time that Musonius, who is reputed to have been the most outstanding philosopher that ever was, was jailed in Nero's prisons. He and Apollonius did not converse with one another openly, since Musonius was opposed to that in case they were both endangered. They conversed, however, by letter through visits of Menippus and Damis to the prison. I will leave aside the letters that concern unimportant subjects, and write down the essential ones and those that give an insight of greatness.[22]

'Apollonius greets Musonius the philosopher.

'I want to come to you and share your conversation and your shelter, in order to do you a favour. If you do not disbelieve the tale of Hercules rescuing Theseus from Hades, write to me what you have decided. Goodbye.'

'Musonius greets Apollonius the philosopher.

'You will have everlasting praise for your plan. But a true man undertakes his defence and shows his innocence. Goodbye.'

'Apollonius to Musonius the philosopher.

'Socrates of Athens preferred not to be rescued by his friends, and so came to court and was executed. Goodbye.'

'Musonius to Apollonius the philosopher.

'Socrates died because he had not prepared to defend himself. I will defend myself. Goodbye.'

47. Nero was departing for Greece, and gave a public pronouncement that no philosopher was to be in Rome. So Apollonius decided to visit the western part of the world, which is said to have the Pillars as its boundary.[23] His intention was to

22. On the letters of Apollonius, see Introduction, pp. 10–11 above.
23. The Pillars (i.e. of Hercules) are the Straits of Gibraltar. The time of Nero's departure for Greece was autumn, A.D. 66.

see the tides of Ocean and Cadiz, and he had also heard about the love of wisdom of the people there and their high degree of sanctity. All his pupils followed him, approving both of the expedition and of Apollonius.

BOOK V

7. Damis says that Apollonius gave many discourses about their experiences there,[1] but these were the ones worth recording. Once they had sat down in the temple of Hercules, when Menippus burst out laughing at the recollection of Nero, and said, 'I wonder how that great man is, and which of the games he has won the prize in, and whether our Greek friends are attending the festivals with endless mirth?'

'According to what I heard from Telesinus,' replied Apollonius, 'the modest Nero is afraid of the Eleans' whips. When his flatterers urged him to win the Olympics and proclaim Rome as the winner, he said, "Yes, unless the Eleans are mean to me. I hear that they use whips and despise me," and he made other more idiotic pronouncements. It is my opinion that Nero will win at Olympia, since no one will have the courage to vote against him, but will not win the Olympics, since they are not being held at the proper time. Last year was the traditional year for them, but Nero ordered the Eleans to postpone them until his visit, as if they were to sacrifice to himself rather than to Zeus. And what do you think of his promising performances in tragedy and on the lyre to men who have neither a theatre nor a stage for this purpose, but merely a natural stadium and bare spaces? Or of his winning a contest one should be ashamed of, and casting off the roles of Augustus and Julius to change instead into those of Amoebeus and Terpnus?[2] What do you think of his being so perfect in the

1. In Baetica (Southern Spain).

2. Amoebeus and Terpnus were both singers to the accompaniment of the cithara (a stringed instrument). Suetonius, Nero 20, mentions Terpnus as a singer at Nero's court.

role of Creon and Oedipus[3] that he is worried he may accidentally get his entrance or his costume or his sceptre wrong? While he is so oblivious of himself and Rome that instead of making measures he is singing them, playing the beggar out of doors when he should be sitting as emperor indoors, managing land and sea. Menippus, there are many actors, whose company Nero is joining: but just suppose one of them left the theatre after playing Oenomaus or Cresphontes,[4] and was so full of his role that he wanted to rule over others and thought himself a tyrant. What would you think of him? Wouldn't you think he needed hellebore and any kind of potion that clears the brain? But imagine the tyrant himself, exchanging his position for that of an actor and an artist, modulating his voice, trembling at Eleans or Delphians, or, if he doesn't, showing such ignorance of his own role that he does not think he will get a whipping from people whose appointed ruler he is. What do you think of the god-forsaken creatures living in the power of such scum? What do you think his effect is on the Greeks, that of Xerxes sacking or Nero singing? If you think of the supplies that they provide for his performances, how they are evicted from their houses, how they cannot maintain any good furniture or slaves for themselves, the terrible things that will happen to their women and children with Nero picking his unspeakable pleasures from every home, all the trials that will arise; one need only mention those trials that concern his audiences and his songs – "you didn't come to hear Nero", "you came but you were distracted", "you laughed", "you didn't clap", "you didn't

3. For Creon and Oedipus, see the three Theban plays of Sophocles.

4. Oenomaus was a king of Pisa, a city of the Peloponnese; he was incestuously in love with his daughter, Hippodameia, whose suitor was Pelops, Tantalus's son. Cresphontes was the leader of a Dorian invasion of the Peloponnese; he took the territory of Messenia for himself. The covert allusions to Nero at Olympia (in the Peloponnese) are easy to detect.

sacrifice on behalf of his voice, with a prayer that he would have even more success with it at Delphi" – don't you think there may be a sea of troubles for the spectators in Greece? And whether the Isthmus will be cut or not (an operation which is now being performed,[5] I gather), that is something I learned long ago from a divine revelation.'

'Well,' Damis replied, 'I think, Apollonius, that this attempt to cut it is the grandest of all Nero's plans; you must agree it's an ambitious scheme.'

'I agree, Damis,' he replied, 'but it will be spoiled by interruption; his singing will be interrupted, and so will his digging. When I think of Xerxes' accomplishments, I admire him not because he bridged the Hellespont but because he crossed it.[6] But I foresee that Nero will not sail through the Isthmus or achieve the completion of his excavation; in fact I think he will leave Greece in an utter panic, if the truth still exists.'

8. Some time later a relay-runner arrived in Cadiz, telling them to sacrifice at good news and sing a hymn to Nero as a triple Olympic winner. Cadiz understood what the victory meant and that there was a celebrated competition in Arcadia, since, as I have mentioned, the inhabitants are fond of Greek customs. But the neighbouring cities had no idea what the Olympics were, or even what a competition or a game was, or why they were sacrificing. They formed absurd ideas, such as that this was a victory in war, and that Nero had captured some people called 'Olympians'. In fact they had never seen a tragedy or a lyre-concert either.

5. Cutting through the Isthmus of Corinth was an unfinished project of Nero; it was later taken up again by the sophist Herodes Atticus.

6. cf. Herodotus, Book VII.

9. The natives of Hipola, which is another city in Baetica,[7] according to Damis were affected by a tragic actor in a way I must mention too. The cities were sacrificing constantly because of Nero's victories, since his Pythian ones had also been reported; and a tragic actor who had decided not to compete with Nero was touring the cities of the west for profit. His skill brought him success among the more civilized, primarily because of the simple fact that he had visited people who had never attended a tragedy, and also because he claimed to be expert in Nero's melodies. But when he reached Hipola, he caused terror even while he remained silent on the stage, and when the poor things saw his great strides and gaping mouth, the high boots he wore, and his strange clothing, they already felt some fear at his appearance. But when he raised his voice with a booming sound, they almost all went running as if an apparition had shouted at them. These are the quaint ways of the barbarians of this region.

10. When the procurator of Baetica professed a desire to meet and converse with him,[8] Apollonius said that those who were not philosophers found his conversation dull. But the man persevered with his request, and since he was said to be virtuous and to take offence at Nero's capers, Apollonius wrote him a letter asking him to come to Cadiz. The man came, leaving aside the dignity of his office, and accompanied only by a few very close friends. The two men exchanged greetings and asked those present to leave: what the subject of their conversation was is absolutely unknown, though Damis guesses that they conspired against Nero, since after

7. Modern Seville.
8. If Philostratus's language is imprecise here, the reference may be to the quaestor of Baetica, A. Caecina Alienus, who was to be active in the revolutions after Nero's death. Elsewhere in Spain (in Tarraconensis) Galba, Nero's successor as emperor, was governor.

three days of conversation alone the procurator left after embracing Apollonius and he replied, 'Goodbye, and remember Vindex.' Now the significance of this was that when Nero was singing in Greece, the western lands are said to have been incited against him by Vindex.[9] This was a man worthy to cut those strings Nero played so badly, since he gave a speech against Nero to the armies in his command, and this speech was of the kind that a very genuine love of wisdom might inspire against a tyrant. Vindex said that Nero was anything rather than a lyre-player, and a lyre-player rather than an emperor. He would blame him for his madness, avarice, savagery and degeneracy of every kind, but would not blame him for his most savage deed, the murder of his mother: that was justified, because she had had such a son.[10] Apollonius foresaw all this, and so endeavoured to make the official of the province next to Vindex's join him, practically taking arms himself in the service of Rome.

11. When the situation in the west became inflamed, the party made for Africa and Etruria. After travelling partly by land, partly by sea, they stopped at Lilybaeum in Sicily. Then they sailed on to Messina and the strait, where the confluence of the Tyrrhenian and the Adriatic seas makes the maelstrom. There, it seems, they were informed that Nero was in exile, Vindex dead, and that people were competing for the power from Rome or from this or that province. Apollonius's disciples asked him what the result would be and who would finally gain power, and he replied, 'Many Thebans.' The short term of domination which Vitellius, Galba and Otho enjoyed made him compare them to the Thebans, who attained mastery over Greece for a very short time.[11]

9. Philostratus's chronology is faulty: cf. Introduction, p. 18 above.
10. Nero had his mother, Agrippina, murdered in A.D. 59.
11. Galba came to the throne in A.D. 68 after Nero's death; he was

12. These predictions he made from divine impulse, and those who think him a magician are wrong in their opinion. That emerges from what has gone before, and there is also this to consider: magicians, who are in my opinion the greatest scoundrels on earth, resort to questioning ghosts or to barbaric sacrifices, or to incantations or anointings, and thus claim to alter fate; and many of them have been induced by accusations to confess skill in such matters. Apollonius, however, followed the warnings of fate, and foretold the way they were sure to come out, and his clairvoyance was due not to magic but to divine revelation. When he saw the tripods and the servers in India and all the other things which I described moving automatically,[12] he did not ask the natives how they had engineered them, and did not ask to be told: he simply praised them without seeing fit to imitate them.

13. When they arrived in Syracuse, there was a woman of quite high rank who had given birth to a monster such as had never been delivered before. The baby had three heads, each on its own neck but the rest of it belonged to a single body. Some interpreted it unintelligently as a sign that Sicily, which has three corners, would be ruined if it did not unite and agree; in fact many of the cities were in internal and external strife, and the art of living at peace had vanished from the island. Others said that Typho, who had many heads, was threatening disaster for Sicily. Apollonius however said, 'Go, Damis, and see if that is the way it is formed,' since the child was exposed publicly for the benefit of those who professed to interpret

---

succeeded in January 69 by Otho, who was in turn succeeded by Vitellius in April. Later in the same year Vitellius was overthrown by Vespasian. The Theban hegemony in Greece had lasted from 371–361 B.C.

12. The description of the Indian dumb-waiters occurs in III. 27 (omitted from this translation).

prodigies. When Damis reported that the child had three heads
and was a boy, Apollonius brought together his disciples and
said: 'There are three emperors of Rome, whom I called
"Thebans" the other day. None of them will complete his
reign. Two will die after ruling in Rome itself, and the other
after ruling in the regions near Rome, all of them throwing off
their masks quicker than the tyrants of tragedy.' His words
immediately came to fulfilment. Galba died after tasting power
in Rome itself, Vitellius died after a mere vision of power, and
Otho was killed in Gaul of the west, not even getting a fine
burial, since he is buried like a private citizen. All these
vicissitudes of fate occurred in one year.

. . . . .

18. Apollonius pursued philosophy in Sicily as long as the
island was sufficiently attentive to him, and then set off for
Greece about the time of Arcturus's rising.[13] The crossing was
uneventful, but when he got to Leucas he said, 'Let us leave
this ship. It would be better for it not to sail to Achaea.'
Nobody paid attention to this remark, except those who knew
Apollonius; so that he sailed in a Leucadian ship with those
who wished to accompany him, and put in at Lechaeum, but
the Syracusan ship sank as it was entering the Crisaean gulf.

19. He was initiated at Athens, with the ceremony performed
by the hierophant whom he had foretold to the man's pre-
decessor.[14] There he met Demetrius the philosopher, who had
lived in Athens since the incident of Nero's bath and his
remarks about it, showing such courage in doing so that he
did not even leave Greece during the time when Nero was
making a mockery of the games. Demetrius said he had seen
Musonius at the Isthmus working in chains and compelled to

13. Mid-September.
14. See IV. 19 above, with note there.

dig. He himself, naturally, had expressed outrage, but Musonius clutched his pickaxe and struck the ground vigorously, and
then stood up and said, 'Does it pain you, Demetrius, to see
me digging the Isthmus for the good of Greece? What would
you have felt if you had seen me playing the lyre like Nero?'[15]
There are other even more admirable remarks of Musonius,
but I had better not mention them. I do not want to be
thought to be drawing an unwise comparison between myself
and the man who made them so offhandedly.

· · · · ·

27. Vespasian set his ambition on the imperial power when he
was in the country bordering Egypt.[16] As he approached it,
people like Dio and Euphrates, whom I shall mention shortly,
encouraged general rejoicing.[17] After the first emperor who
set the affairs of Rome in order,[18] harsh tyrannies had lasted for
fifty years, so that even Claudius, who ruled for thirteen years
in the middle of this period, did not seem virtuous. It is true
that he entered power at the age of fifty, when men's intelligence is at its highest, and he was thought to be devoted to
culture of every kind. Even he, however, at his age often had
childish ideas and let women usurp his power; and so carelessly
did he allow them to murder him that, though he knew what
was going to happen to him, he took no precautions against
his foreknowledge.

15. In the preserved writings of Lucian there is a short dialogue
entitled 'Nero or Cutting through the Isthmus', in which Musonius is
an interlocutor. The dialogue is not by Lucian; some think Philostratus
the biographer wrote it.

16. Judaea, where Vespasian was leading Roman forces against the
Jews.

17. Dio is the celebrated philosopher and rhetor of the later first
century A.D., Dio of Prusa (called Chrysostom, 'golden-mouthed').
Euphrates was another philosopher of the period; Pliny the Younger
mentions him in his letters (I. 10).

18. Caesar Augustus (27 B.C.–A.D. 14).

Apollonius was no less pleased than Euphrates and Dio about these events, but he did not make them the subject of public speeches, considering that style of speaking more the business of professionals. When the emperor approached, he was met before the gates by the priests, the officials of Egypt, and the governors of the 'nomes' into which Egypt is parcelled,[19] and by philosophers and every kind of wise man. Apollonius, however, did not take part in any of this ceremonial, but stayed conversing in the temple. The emperor spoke to people gently and kindly, and after a short address said, 'Is the man from Tyana here?'

'Yes,' they answered, 'he has made us better men.'

'Is there some way he might join us?' the emperor asked; 'I greatly wish to meet him.'

Dio replied, 'He will meet you at the temple, since that is what he arranged with me when I arrived here.'

'Let us go there,' said the emperor, 'to pray to the gods and meet a virtuous man.'

That gave rise to a story to the effect that Vespasian had had the idea of seizing power when he was besieging Jerusalem, and he had sent for Apollonius to advise him on this: but Apollonius had refused to enter a country whose inhabitants defiled it by what they did and allowed to be done to them. From here the emperor was supposed to have come after achieving power in order to have the conversation with Apollonius that I am going to relate.

28. After sacrificing, and before he had properly attended to the cities, he addressed Apollonius, and as if he was praying to him said, 'Make me emperor.'

'I have done so,' was the reply, 'because I previously prayed for an emperor who was just, generous and moderate, with

19. 'Nomes' were Egyptian administrative districts, taken over by the Romans from the Ptolemaic organization of Egypt.

becoming white hair, and the father of legitimate children; and it is clear that you are the answer to my prayers.'

The emperor was delighted by this, and the crowd in the sanctuary also cheered, agreeing with Apollonius's words.

'What was your opinion of Nero's reign?' Vespasian asked.

'Perhaps Nero knew how to tune a lyre,' replied Apollonius, 'but he disgraced his reign by letting it go flat and then making it too sharp.'

'Is it your advice that a ruler should be balanced, then?'

'Not mine, but god's, who has defined balance as equality. On this subject you have good advisers in these men,' pointing to Dio and Euphrates, who had not yet quarrelled with him. Then the emperor held up his hands and said, 'Zeus, may I rule wise men, and wise men rule me.' And turning to the Egyptians he said, 'Draw as freely from me as you do from the Nile.'

29. Thus Egypt recovered, when oppression had already driven it to despair. Vespasian, however, as he left the sanctuary took Apollonius by the hand and, after leading him to the palace, said, 'Some people perhaps think me a fool for grasping at empire when I am about sixty, so I will defend myself and hope that you will do the same for me to others.

'I do not remember that I was ever tempted by wealth even in my youth, and I behaved with such moderation and reasonableness in the offices and honours that the Roman empire confers that I was never thought either proud or timid. Nor did I ever plan rebellion against Nero. Because he had at least inherited his power from an emperor, even if not lawfully, I obeyed him for the sake of Claudius who made me consul and his adviser.[20] I swear that whenever I saw Nero

20. Vespasian's career advanced notably under Claudius, with the patronage of the emperor's freedman Narcissus. The consulate of Vespasian came in A.D. 51.

misbehaving, I wept to think of Claudius and what scum he had left his greatest possession to. I saw, too, that even when Nero was out of the way human affairs did not change for the better, and the empire was in such a degraded state that it was now in Vitellius's power. So at that point I picked up courage to seize it, first because I want to do a great service to mankind and second because I shall have a playboy for a rival. Vitellius washes more in perfume than I do in water, and in fact I think that if he were struck with a sword he would produce perfume rather than blood. He adds debauch to debauch like a maniac, and when he gambles he dreads that the dice may fall badly for him, while he hazards the empire for fun. He is a woman to whores and a stallion to married women, on the principle that sex is more enjoyable when dangerous. I will not mention his more debauched practices, so as not to speak of such things in front of you; but I hope I may not let the Romans be ruled by such a man, and instead that I may make the gods my guides and prove worthy of myself.

'That is why, Apollonius, I attach myself to you, because they say that you understand the gods more than anybody. I am making you my adviser for concerns that affect land and sea. My hope is that if the gods show their favour, I may continue on this course, but if they do the opposite and are not on my side or the Roman people's, I may stop bothering them against their will.'

30. Apollonius blessed his speech, and said, 'Capitoline Zeus, you, I know, are the judge of the present circumstances. Keep yourself unchanged for this man's good, and him unchanged for yours, since it is decreed that your temple which the hands of the wicked burned yesterday will be restored by this man.'

The emperor was amazed at these words, and Apollonius said, 'These things will reveal themselves. Do not ask me anything, but continue in the way you have rightly planned.'

Now in Rome at that very time Domitian the son of Vespasian was battling with Vitellius to secure his father's power, and had been held under siege in the Capitol. He escaped his besiegers, but the temple was burned,[21] as Apollonius perceived much sooner than if it had happened in Egypt. After this conversation Apollonius left the emperor, saying that the customs of India did not allow him to perform anything at noon which they did not perform themselves. Vespasian was even more encouraged, and he decided not to let fortune slip away, and instead grasped it, trusting from what he had heard that it was assured and already in his power.

31. The next day Apollonius came to the palace about daybreak and asked the guards what the emperor was doing. They replied that he had been up for a long time, and was busy with his correspondence. When Apollonius heard this, he went away, saying to Damis, 'This man will be a ruler.' He returned at sunrise and found Dio and Euphrates at the door. They questioned him eagerly about his conversation with the emperor, and so Apollonius described the defence that the emperor had given him, though without mentioning his own opinions. Apollonius was called in first, and said, 'Emperor, your old acquaintances Euphrates and Dio are at the door. They have your affairs at heart, so call them in too to join our discussion, since they are both wise.'

'I keep my doors unlocked to wise men,' the emperor replied, 'but to you I think even my heart is open.'

32. When they had been called in, the emperor said, 'Gentlemen, I gave the excellent Apollonius a defence of my intentions yesterday.'

'We have heard your defence,' said Dio; 'it was sensible.'

'Well, my dear Dio,' said the emperor, 'today let us discuss

21. cf. Tacitus, *Histories* III. 69–71.

my plans together. I want to do everything with all possible honour and for the good of mankind. I think first of Tiberius and how he allowed his rule to become inhuman and cruel; then of his successor Gaius, and the way he raved and wore oriental dress and won non-existent wars, making a disgusting revel of the whole government of Rome; then of the virtuous Claudius, and how he found women so irresistible that he forgot to rule, or even to stay alive, since they killed him (so it is said). And why should I attack Nero, when Apollonius has already made a brief and pertinent remark about the "flats and sharps" with which he disgraced his rule? Why should I mention the arrangements of Galba, who died in the middle of the forum after adopting Otho and Piso whom he had slept with? And if we were to give the power to Vitellius, the most profligate of them all, Nero would come alive again. I can see, gentlemen, that the tyrannies I have mentioned have brought power into disrepute, and I want your advice about managing it now that it has become abhorrent to mankind.'

To this Apollonius said, 'There was a very expert flute-player who used to send his pupils to less good flute-players so that they would learn how not to play. Well, you have learned how not to rule, emperor, from these wicked rulers. Let us then consider how you ought to rule.'

33. Euphrates was already secretly jealous of Apollonius, see-ing the emperor paying more attention to him than those who travel to oracles do to them. At this point he broke the bounds of moderation, and raising his voice unusually loud, he said, 'It is wrong to flatter people's impulses and to be carried away like fools when they tug at the reins: instead we should check them, if we are philosophers. Whether this course is right is the very question we should have considered in our discus-sion: you are asking us to say how it should be carried out before you have determined whether what we are discussing

is proper. My advice is that Vitellius should be deposed, since I know he is corrupt and drunk with every kind of vice. However, I also know that you are a man of virtue and exceptional probity, and I do not think you should punish Vitellius without knowing yourself. The crimes of autocracy you do not need to discover from me, having described them yourself. But you ought to know this. When youth usurps tyranny, it acts characteristically, tyranny being as natural to the young as getting drunk or making love; a young tyrant is not evil in himself unless he proves murderous, cruel and debauched compared to other tyrants. But if an old man reaches a tyrant's position, the first charge against him is that he desired it. Even if he turns out generous and self-controlled, people will not think these are qualities of the man himself but of his age and maturity: they will think that he desired that position long ago, even as a young man, but failed to achieve it. And such failures also carry the imputation of ill luck or cowardice, since a man is thought either to have put aside his dreams of tyranny because he mistrusted his luck, or to have yielded to another's desire for power because he feared the other's courage.

'Leaving aside the subject of ill luck, how will you defend yourself against the charge of cowardice, especially if you are thought to have feared Nero, the greatest coward and sluggard of them all? The plot that Vindex formed against him should have stirred you, heaven knows, first of all: you had an army, and the forces you were leading against the Jews would have been better employed punishing Nero. The Jews rebelled long ago not only against Rome but against all mankind; people who have devised an unsociable way of life, with no food, libations, prayers or sacrifices in common with other men are further away from us than Susa, Bactria, and the Indians beyond that, so that there was no point in punishing them for rebelling – it would have been better if they had never been conquered. But as for Nero, which of us wouldn't have prayed to kill him with our own hand? He virtually drank human blood, and sang at the same time as he murdered. At any rate my ears were always open for the rumours about you. Whenever somebody came from there, saying that you had caused the deaths of thirty thousand Jews, and fifty thousand in the next battle, I would take the new arrival aside and ask him quietly, "What about the man himself? Isn't he too great for such things?" But since you have decided that Vitellius is the image of Nero and are making war on him, carry out your plan, since it is an honourable one. But thereafter, understand this. Democracy deserves well of Rome, and many of their present possessions they got under that form of constitution. Put an end to autocracy, about which you had such harsh things to say; grant the Romans the favour of popular rule and yourself the favour of inaugurating their liberty.'

34. When Euphrates had said this, Apollonius saw that Dio agreed with his opinion, since that appeared from his nodding and the way he praised him as he spoke. So he said, 'Dio, do you have something to add to what has been said?'

'Yes,' he replied, 'and it is partly similar, and partly dissimilar. The contention that you, emperor, would have done better by deposing Nero than by punishing the Jews is something that I think that I too have said to you. But you seemed to be trying with all your might not to depose him, since anybody who put his confused affairs in good order was strengthening the man against all those whom otherwise he would have been weak against. But I approve of the plan against Vitellius, because in my opinion it is a smaller achievement to overthrow an established tyranny than to prevent one even coming into existence. Now I think highly of democracy; it is a constitution inferior perhaps to aristocracy, but preferable to tyrannies and oligarchies, at least in sensible people's opinions. But I am afraid that these tyrannies have already broken the spirit of the Romans, and will make the change difficult, so that they will prove unable to be free or to face democracy, like people coming out of darkness and looking at full daylight. It is right, therefore, so I think, to force Vitellius out of power, and I hope it happens as quickly and as honourably as possible. I think you should make preparations to make war on him, not however threatening him with war but with punishment if he refuses to abdicate. If you defeat him, as I think you will manage to do without effort, let the Romans choose their own constitution. If they choose democracy, let them have it: that would do you more credit than many tyrannies and many victories at Olympia; your name will be inscribed all over the city, your statue will be set up in bronze, and you will give us a subject for speeches such as neither Harmodius nor Aristogeiton will be compared to.[22] If the Romans were to prefer monarchy, who is left for them all to vote power to except you? For they will surely give you, rather than someone else, what you are handing over from your own power to the public.'

35. This was followed by a silence in which the emperor's face showed the indecision in his mind, because after having behaved and acted like an emperor, it appeared that he was being advised against his plan. Apollonius then said, 'I think you are wrong to change an emperor's mind on a subject already decided; this is puerile babble, when the times demand something more practical. If it was I that had acquired power as great as this man's, and was wondering what good I should do to mankind, and you gave me advice, your words would have had an effect, since the opinions of philosophers sway the

22. Harmodius and Aristogeiton were famed as liberators of Athens from the tyranny of the Peisistratids in the sixth century B.C.

philosophers among their hearers. But you are advising a consular, a man used to rule, who is sure to be ruined if he loses his power. So what point is there in blaming him for not refusing the offer of chance, but accepting it when it is made, when he wants advice on how to use his prize properly? Suppose we saw a tall and courageous athlete with a well proportioned body, and we went up to him when he was already on the road through Arcadia to Olympia and encouraged him to meet his competitors, at the same time advising him not to accept the victory when he won the Olympics and not to allow the olive crown to be put on his head. We would seem to be talking nonsense, or making fun of the efforts of others. Similarly, let us remember who this man is, all the troops he has with him, all the flashing bronze, and the great number of horses, and how noble and self-controlled he is, and how well suited to achieve his aims. Let us then send him on his chosen course with words of good omen and with more favourable advice.

'You seem also to have forgotten that this man is the father of two sons already commanding armies. If he does not hand his power over to them, they will be his bitterest enemies, and he will be reduced to making war on his own family. But if he accepts power, he will be served by his own sons, and they will support him and he them. They will be his bodyguards, not paid ones, of course, or drafted, or the kind that assume a friendly expression, but genuinely well-disposed and faithful.

'I do not care for any constitution, since I live in the power of the gods. But I do not think the human herd ought to be ruined for lack of a just and reasonable shepherd. Just as one man of exceptional virtue changes democracy so that it appears as the rule of one man, the best citizen, so the rule of one man who is always looking after the common good is a democracy.

'He says that you did not depose Nero. But did you,

Euphrates? Did Dio? Did I? But even so no one blames us for that. No one thinks we are cowards if we failed to get a name for acting on behalf of liberty, though philosophers have deposed thousands of tyrannies in the past. In fact for myself I did try to oppose Nero. I was often critical of him in conversation, I censured the monster Tigellinus to his face, and by helping Vindex in the western regions I was fortifying him against Nero.[23] But that will not make me claim that I overthrew the tyrant, and if you did not do the same I will not consider you too cowardly to be true philosophers. Now a philosopher will say what occurs to him, though taking care no doubt not to say anything idiotic or wild. But a consular who plans to depose a tyrant first of all needs a lot of deliberation in order to intervene unexpectedly, and second he needs a suitable excuse to prevent him from appearing disloyal. He is going to use his weapons against the very man who made him general and to whose best interest he swore to dedicate his purposes and actions. He needs, then, to begin by convincing the gods that he is breaking his oath without impiety. He needs many friends, as such a step cannot be taken without defence and protection. He needs a great deal of money to win over the powerful, especially since he is attacking the man who owns the whole world. And these things require endless effort and endless time. You can think what you like of this scheme, since it is not our business to criticize an ambition which he may indeed have had, but in which he received no help from fortune, as he received none even when he had begun the struggle. Since he was only yesterday a ruler, crowned by the cities in the temples here, governing honourably and generously, how will you justify your advice to him to make a public announcement today to the effect that he will be a private citizen in future and was out of his mind when he assumed power? By completing his design he will make willing

23. See above, V. 10.

helpers out of the men he trusted when he conceived it, and equally if he resorts to going back on his decision he will have an enemy in everybody whom he distrusted previously.'

36. The emperor was pleased to hear this, and said, 'If you lived in my own soul, you could not have expressed my feelings so clearly. I accept your advice, because I believe every word that comes from you is inspired. So tell me everything a good emperor should do.'

Apollonius replied, 'What you ask, emperor, cannot be taught; kingship is the most important thing in human affairs, and yet no one can teach it. But I will certainly tell you what I think is the proper course for you to take.

'Do not consider real wealth to be the kind that is stored away, since that is no better than sand piled up from here and there, nor the kind that is sent to you by people who groan over their tribute, because gold is adulterated and discoloured if it comes from the tears of mankind. You would make better use of gold than any ruler if you helped the needy and guaranteed for the rich the safe enjoyment of their wealth. Your unlimited licence is something you should respect; that way you will use it sensibly. Do not cut down the tallest and most prominent of the stalks, because this advice of Aristotle's is unjust;[24] instead, uproot ill will like thistles from corn; deter rebels not with the punishments you do give but with those you might give. The law, emperor, must rule you too; since you will be more prudent in the administration of the laws if you do not despise them.

'Worship the gods more than you have in the past, since they have given you a great present, and it is for a great empire that you make your prayers. Act like an emperor in matters that concern your power, but like an ordinary citizen

24. Aristotle, *Politics* III. 1284a 26ff. and V. 1311a 20ff.

in matters that concern your person. Gambling, drink, sex, and the avoidance of such things I do not need to advise you about, since you did not approve of them even in your youth, so it is said.

'You have two sons, emperor, who I hear are excellent.[25] Make them of all people your subjects, because their faults will certainly reflect on you. Be ready to use the threat that you will not leave them the throne if they turn out not to remain honest and good: that will make them think of the throne not as an heirloom but a reward for virtue.

'There are many pleasures which are endemic at Rome, and it is my advice, emperor, that you check them without using extremes. It is difficult to convert a people to complete temperance; you have to make their minds accustomed to control little by little, by both direct and indirect constraint. Let us have no more extravagance in the slaves and freedmen that come with the throne, but make them used to a humbler attitude, just as they now have a greater master.

'It only remains to mention the governors that are sent regularly to the provinces. I do not mean the ones you send yourself, since you will surely give commands according to excellence, but the ones who receive power by lot.[26] It is my opinion that those who are sent should be suitable for the countries they are assigned to, as far as the lot allows. Greek-speakers should rule Greeks, Latin-speakers should rule those who share their language and are suitable. I will tell you what has given me this conviction. At the time I was staying in the

25. The two sons were the future emperors Titus and Domitian. Titus enjoyed wide popularity both before and while he was emperor. As a boy, Domitian was well known for his modest blush, which little betokened the subsequent cruelty and tyranny of his reign.

26. The provinces of the Roman empire were divided between those (imperial provinces) to which the emperor appointed governors and those (senatorial provinces) for which governors were chosen by lot. There was obviously some possibility of manipulation of the lot.

Peloponnese, the man ruling Greece did not know Greek customs, and the Greeks had no understanding of him either. As a result, he usually did wrong and was done wrong, because his advisers and assessors when he gave judgement in court sold his verdicts and treated the governor like a slave.

'That is all that has occurred to me for today, emperor. If something else strikes me, we will converse again. Now get on with the business that your position involves, if you don't want to be thought lazy by your subjects.'

37. Euphrates then said, 'I do not oppose what you have already decided: what good would I do trying to make you change your mind? But as for philosophy, emperor (since that is your title now), I advise you to approve and pursue the kind that is in accordance with nature. But avoid the kind that claims to be inspired: people like that lie about the gods, and urge us to do many foolish things.'

This was an allusion to Apollonius, but he, without even turning around, left with his pupils now that the interview was over. Euphrates then wanted to say something even more ill-considered about him, but the emperor, seeing his intention and wanting to get rid of him, said, 'Admit those who have requests to make of the government, and let my council resume its usual form.' In this way Euphrates did not realize that he had injured his reputation, since the emperor now thought him malicious and unprincipled, and considered him to have spoken as he did about democracy not from conviction but to contradict Apollonius and his opinions about the empire. Even so, the emperor did not disown Euphrates or reveal any annoyance at what had happened. He did not approve of Dio either for backing Euphrates's opinions, but still kept his affection for him. Dio was a graceful talker, who avoided quarrels and had a charm in his speech like the perfume that comes from a temple: and he also had the gift of extraordinary improvisation.

But Apollonius not only had the emperor's affection: he entranced him with his description of ancient customs, his accounts of the Indian Phraotes, his tales of the rivers and the animals that are found in India, and all the predictions about the empire that he received from divine revelation. When Vespasian was about to leave Egypt, now that it was settled and restored, he wanted to take Apollonius on his journey. Apollonius declined, on the ground that he had not yet seen the full extent of Egypt or conversed with the Naked Philosophers, though he was extremely eager to compare Egyptian wisdom with Indian. 'And I have not yet drunk from the Nile at its source,' he said. The emperor realized that he was preparing to travel to Ethiopia, and said, 'You will remember me, won't you?'

'Of course,' was the reply, 'if you remain a good emperor and remember yourself.'

. . . . . .

41. I want to show why he never visited the emperor again or met him after the incident in Egypt, even though Vespasian invited him and very often wrote to him with this request from wherever he happened to be.

Nero, by a decision of uncharacteristic wisdom, had given Greece its liberty, so that the cities went back to their Doric and Attic customs, and there was prosperity everywhere as well as concord in the cities, which there had not been even in ancient Greece.[27] Vespasian, however, on his arrival there deprived Greece of this gift, giving as his reason their faction

27. Nero's speech, in which he proclaimed the liberation of the Hellenes from Roman rule, is preserved on an inscription from Boeotia in Greece. The liberation took place in November A.D. 67 (or just possibly 66).

and other matters which certainly did not deserve this degree of anger.[28] This seemed out of character with the mildness of his rule not only to those it affected but to Apollonius too, and so he wrote to the emperor as follows.

'Apollonius greets the emperor Vespasian.

'You have enslaved Greece, I am told. You think you have a greater prize than Xerxes, but do not realize that you have a lesser one than Nero, since Nero had the prize but declined it. Goodbye.'

'Apollonius to the same.

'If you are on such bad terms with the Greeks as to turn them from free men into slaves, what need do you have of my presence? Goodbye.'

'Apollonius to the same.

'Nero freed the Greeks in play, but you have enslaved them in earnest. Goodbye.'

This then was what made Apollonius offended with Vespasian. But when he heard how well he conducted his whole reign thereafter, he made no secret of his pleasure and of his belief that he too shared in the benefaction.

42. Apollonius did another thing in Egypt that was considered a miracle. There was a man who had a tame lion on a lead like a dog, and the creature was friendly not only to its master but to anybody it met. It went begging from city to city, and was even admitted to shrines because of its abstemiousness: it never licked up sacrificial blood or pounced on the victims when they were being flayed and slaughtered, and instead lived on honey-cakes, bread, sweetmeats and cooked meat, and it could also be seen drinking wine without losing its gentleness.

28. Vespasian's cancellation of the Greek freedom came early in his reign. He said that the Greeks had forgotten how to be free (Pausanias VII. 17. 2 [4]).

This creature came up to Apollonius when he was sitting in the sanctuary, nuzzled his knees, and begged from him more than from anybody. Everyone else thought it wanted a reward, but Apollonius said, 'The lion wants me to tell you the human whose soul it has: well, this is Amasis, the former king of Egypt in the Saite district.' When the lion heard this, it gave a pathetic, mournful roar, and lay down sobbing, actually shedding tears. Apollonius stroked it and said, 'I advise you to send the lion to Leontopolis to be the sacred property of the sanctuary: a king who has turned into the most kingly of animals should not have to scrounge like a human beggar, in my opinion.' So the priests assembled to sacrifice to Amasis, and dressing the animal up with a collar and ribbons escorted it up country, with piping and singing of hymns and songs composed in its honour.

43. Apollonius had now had enough of Alexandria, and so prepared to leave for Egypt and Ethiopia to meet the Naked Philosophers. Because Menippus was now able to conduct a discussion and was formidable in repartee, Apollonius left him behind to take over the struggle with Euphrates; and he dissuaded Dioscorides from the journey, seeing that he was not enthusiastic about the trip. Then he assembled the rest, because many others had joined him after those that had deserted at Aricia, and gave them a lecture about the trip, beginning in this way:

'I have to make an Olympic announcement to you, my friends; and an Olympic announcement goes like this. When an athlete comes for the Olympics, the Eleans let him practise for thirty days in Elis itself. Then they bring the athletes together and, unlike the Delphians at the Pythian games and the Corinthians at the Isthmian ones who say, "Proceed to the stadium, and prove yourselves to be men who deserve to win," the Eleans address the athletes as follows when they come to

Olympia: "If your efforts are worthy of your coming to Olympia, and you have not shown any laziness or degeneracy, proceed with confidence. But those of you who have not had this training may go your own ways.'"

His disciples understood his speech, and twenty of them stayed with Menippus. But others, numbering ten I think, after praying to the gods and making the sacrifice appropriate for a kind of embarkation, immediately started for the pyramids on camels and with the Nile on their right. They also sailed across the river at many points in order to learn about everything on it, and there was no city, sanctuary, or any sacred place in Egypt that they passed in silence, but always they gave and received instruction through a kind of holy conversation, and every ship that Apollonius sailed in was like a sacred galley.

BOOK VI

———

1. Ethiopia constitutes the western promontory of the whole world, as India does of the eastern; it borders Egypt at Meroe, includes a part of unexplored Africa, and ends at the sea which the poets call the Ocean, since that is their name for what encircles the earth. Ethiopia supplies Egypt with the river Nile, which rises at the Cataracts and brings from Ethiopia all the soil with which it floods Egypt. In size this land cannot be compared with India, as indeed none of the other continents that are famous among men can; even if we were to join all of Egypt with Ethiopia, as we must consider the river does, the two of them, compared with so large a country as India, are still not equal to it in size. The rivers of the two continents are alike when one considers the behaviour of the Indus and the Nile. They irrigate the continents in summer, when the earth most needs it, and they are the only rivers to produce the crocodile and the hippopotamus; they are equally famous for their sacred sites, since many of the sacred beliefs the Indians hold about their river are also held about the Nile. The similarity of the two continents may also be considered to be shown by the spices there, by the lions and the fact that elephants are caught and trained in both. They also produce beasts seen nowhere else, and black men, as no other continents do, and they contain tribes of Pygmies and of humans that bark in various ways, and other amazing things of that kind. Indian griffins and Ethiopian ants may be of different shape, but they seem to have the same pursuits, because both are celebrated on the two continents as hoarders of gold and for favouring the gold-producing regions. But that is enough

on these topics; my story must return to its proper subject
and concern itself with Apollonius.

2. He arrived at the crossing-point between Ethiopia and
Egypt, which is called Sycamore. There he saw uncoined
bullion, linen, ivory, roots, perfume and spices, all lying unguarded at a fork in the road. I will explain the meaning of
this, since the custom is observed to this day. The Ethiopians
bring goods consisting of their country's products, all of
which the Egyptians carry away, while they bring Egyptian
goods of equal value to the same place, using what they have
to buy what they lack. Those who live at the border of the
two countries are not exactly black but of the same colour
as each other, less black than the Ethiopians but more so than
the Egyptians.

Apollonius, understanding the method of the exchange,
said, 'Contrast the honourable Greeks. They think life not
worth living unless one penny produces another, and they
can force up the price of goods for each other by retailing or
hoarding. One man gives as his excuse that his daughter is of
marriageable age, another that his son is entering manhood,
another that he has to pay his club-dues, another that he
is building a house, another that he would be ashamed
to be thought less good in business than his father. It
was a happy situation when wealth was not honoured,
equality reigned, "dark iron was hidden away"[1] because
mankind was united, and the whole world was considered
one.'

3. This was the way he conversed, characteristically taking his
cue for each lecture from circumstances. They proceeded

1. cf. Hesiod, *Works and Days*, 160. Philostratus's text is a slight
misquotation.

towards Memnon,[2] guided by an Egyptian boy of whom Damis gives the following account.

This boy's name was Timasion. He was just passing out of his teens and still had his boyish physique. He was well behaved, but his step-mother had been in love with him, and had persecuted him by turning his father against him. Using a trick that even Phaedra had refrained from,[3] she gave out that he was effeminate and liked male lovers more than female. The boy left Naucratis, which was where all this had happened, and lived near Memphis; he bought a ship, equipped it at his own expense, and plied it on the Nile. He saw Apollonius sailing up river when he was sailing down, and realized that the passengers were wise men from their philosophers' cloaks and the attention they gave to their books. He begged them to let him share their journey, because he loved wisdom, whereupon Apollonius said, 'This is a well-behaved boy, my friends. He should be granted what he asks.' He then related the story about the step-mother to those of his companions nearby, speaking in a low voice while the boy's boat was still approaching. When the boats met, Timasion came

2. At Thebes in Egypt there were two colossal seated figures which commemorated the dead Amenophis of the eighteenth dynasty. One of these colossi was partially toppled by an earthquake in about 26 B.C., and it appears that the remaining part thenceforth emitted a sound, like the breaking of a harpstring, every morning at sunrise. The earthquake damage evidently allowed air to penetrate well inside the colossus in such a way that the sudden warmth of the sun at dawn effected a noisy discrepancy between the quickly heated exterior and the still cool channels within. The sounding colossus was a great tourist attraction under the Roman Empire; the Greeks of that age identified it with the mythical hero, Memnon. At the end of the second century A.D. Septimius Severus repaired the statue, it is alleged, and thereby silenced it.

3. Phaedra was stricken with love for her stepson Hippolytus. Her infatuation and its tragic consequences are the subject of Euripides's play, *Hippolytus*, as well as of Seneca's *Phaedra* and Racine's *Phèdre*.

across, and after giving some instruction to his own steersman about the cargo addressed Apollonius and his company.

Apollonius asked him to sit in front of him, and said, 'Young man from Egypt (you look as if you are a native), tell me what you have done that is bad or good, and I will excuse you from the bad because of your age, and praise you for the good, so that you can become a follower of wisdom with myself and these men.' Seeing Timasion blush and move his lips, uncertain whether to speak or not, Apollonius kept pressing his question as if he had no foreknowledge about him, until Timasion plucked up courage and said, 'Gods above, how am I to describe myself? I am not wicked, but I am not sure I should be called good, because avoiding wrong is no praise in itself.'

'Goodness,' said Apollonius, 'you talk as if you were from India, young man. The inspired Iarchas had your very opinion. But tell us how you came to have this belief, and how long ago. I have the impression that you are avoiding some crime.'

The boy began to tell how his step-mother had made advances to him, and he had left because of her passion. At that there was a shout, because Apollonius's prediction had been miraculous. But Timasion said in response, 'Gentlemen, what is this? What I have said is as far from being amazing as it is from being funny.'

Damis replied, 'Something else that you do not know of yet surprised us. But we also praise you, young man, because you don't think you have done anything extraordinary.'

'Do you sacrifice to Aphrodite, my boy?' asked Apollonius.

'Certainly,' said the boy, 'every day. She is a goddess who I think has great power in the affairs of men and gods.'

Apollonius was delighted, and said, 'My friends, let us vote him a crown for his self-control, which exceeds that of Hippolytus the son of Theseus. He insulted Aphrodite, which perhaps saved him from yielding to sexual desires or ever feeling the ravages of love, but it made him rather boorish and heartless in character. This boy, by contrast, admits that he served the goddess but was unaffected by the woman's desires; he preferred to go away from her, afraid of what the goddess would do if he did not avoid another's sinful passion. In fact I do not think it a sign of self-control to be on bad terms with any god, as Hippolytus was with Aphrodite. It shows better control to speak well of every god, especially at Athens where there are altars set up to unknown gods.'[4]

That was his discourse about Timasion, though he did call him 'Hippolytus' because of the way he had eyed his stepmother, and the boy also seemed to have cultivated his physique and to have taken exercise to increase his appeal.

4. With this boy's guidance they apparently reached the sanctuary of Memnon, about whom Damis gives this account. He was the son of Dawn, and did not fall at Troy, in fact he did not even go there, but died in Ethiopia, after ruling it for five generations. The Ethiopians are the longest-lived people on earth; they mourn for Memnon as one who died very young, and they weep over his premature death. The place where his statue is apparently resembles an ancient market-place, like the deserted market-places in cities inhabited long ago, which have shattered monuments, crumbling walls, seats, doorways, and ornamental herms that have been destroyed either by human agency or by time.

The statue itself faces the sun, and represents a young man still beardless. It is of dark stone, with both its feet together, in the style of Daedalus's statues, and with its arms straight and pressed down on its throne in the attitude of a sitting man just about to stand up. This position, the look in its eyes, and the famous expression of its lips, as if it was about to speak,

4. cf. *Acts of the Apostles* XVII. 23.

seem not to have particularly impressed the party most of the time, because they still looked lifeless. But when the sun's ray hit the statue at sunrise, they could not withhold their amazement: the statue made a sound the moment the ray fell on its lips, and its eyes appeared to gaze cheerfully at the light, as the eyes of sunbathers do. At that point, it seems, the party realized that the statue seemed to be rising in honour of the Sun, like people who stand to worship the powers above. They sacrificed to the Sun of Ethiopia and Memnon of the Dawn, as the priests instructed them; they give these titles to the sun because he 'heats' and 'glows', to Memnon because of his mother.⁵ The party then travelled on to the region of the Naked Philosophers.

5. They met a man dressed like a Memphite, who seemed to be wandering about rather than going in any direction. Damis and the others asked him who he was and why he was straying. Timasion then said, 'Ask me, not him. He would not tell you what has happened to him because he is ashamed of the unhappy state he is in. But I know the man and pity him, and will tell you his whole story. He killed a Memphite by accident and the laws of Memphis order a man who goes (as he has to do) into exile for an accidental crime to stay with the Naked Philosophers. If he is purified of his murder he can at last return to society purified, though first he has to visit the murdered man's tomb and make some small sacrifice there. But in the time before he has met with the Naked Philosophers he has to wander about in this border area, until they take compassion on him like a suppliant.'

5. Philostratus sees in the word 'Ethiopia' an etymological connexion with the Greek verbs *aithō* (to burn or blaze) and *thalpō* (to warm). The translator has tried to suggest the same sort of connexion in English by his phrase 'heats and glows'. According to legend, Memnon was the son of Dawn by Tithonus.

Apollonius asked Timasion what opinion the Naked Philosophers had about this outcast, but he replied, 'I don't know. He has been a suppliant here for six months without yet being purified.'

'The men you mention are not wise,' said Apollonius, 'if they do not absolve him, or realize that Philiscus, who was this man's victim, was descended from Thamus the Egyptian who once pillaged the Naked Philosophers' region.'

Timasion was amazed. 'What are you saying?' he asked.

'The truth, my boy,' said Apollonius. 'Thamus once plotted revolution in Memphis, but the Naked Philosophers exposed him and stopped him. So, disappointed in his aim, he began to pillage all their cultivated lands, since he controlled the land round Memphis by brigandage. I see that Philiscus, who was killed by this man, was Thamus's descendant in the thirteenth generation, and so was obviously a sworn enemy of these Philosophers, whose land Thamus ravaged at that time. They ought to have crowned this man even if he had killed Philiscus deliberately, and there is no wisdom in refusing to absolve him for a murder that was accidental but to their advantage.'

The boy was stunned, and said, 'Stranger, who are you?'

Apollonius replied, 'You will find out among the Naked Philosophers. But it is absolutely forbidden for me to address a man with blood-guilt, so tell him to be cheerful, young man: he will receive immediate absolution if he comes to where I am staying.'

When the man arrived, Apollonius performed all the rites of purification prescribed by Empedocles and Pythagoras, and then told the man to return to society: he was now free from guilt.

6. They set out from there at sunrise, and before noon reached the Naked Philosophers' place of meditation. These Naked

Philosophers apparently live on a hill of moderate height a little distance from the bank of the Nile. In wisdom the Indians surpass them to a greater degree than they themselves surpass the Egyptians. They go naked except for garments like those of sunbathers at Athens. There are a few trees in their enclosure and a rather small grove where they gather to discuss community affairs. Their sanctuaries are not built in one place, like the Indians', but in different places on the hill, and are highly regarded, so the Egyptians say. They worship the Nile particularly, because they consider it to be earth and water. For themselves they do not need huts or houses, and live out under the open sky, but they have built a shelter, sufficient to house their visitors, in the form of a fairly small colonnade about the length of the ones at Elis in which the athletes wait for the announcement at noon.

7. At this point Damis recounts a trick of Euphrates which should be regarded not merely as silly but disgraceful by the standards of philosophy. He had heard Apollonius many times express a wish to compare Indian and Egyptian wisdom. He therefore sent Thrasybulus of Naucratis to the Naked Philosophers to slander Apollonius. Thrasybulus said that he had come to converse with them and that the man from Tyana was coming too. This promised no small trouble for them, he said, because Apollonius was wiser than the sages of India, whom he extolled in every conversation, and had devised endless tests for the Naked Philosophers; he himself was no inferior to the sun or sky or the earth, because he could move and transport them to any new place he wanted.

8. When the man from Naucratis had hatched his plot, he left, while the Naked Philosophers believed him entirely. When Apollonius arrived, they did not refuse an interview but pretended that they were attending to important affairs

which were occupying them; they would, however, come to talk with him if they had time and were informed what he wanted and what his aim was in coming. Their messenger also invited the party to stay in the colonnade, to which Apollonius replied, 'You do not need to mention shelter, because the climate here is such that nobody needs a covering' (this was a hint that they went naked not out of asceticism but necessity). 'However, I am not surprised that these people do not yet know what I want and why I have come: the Indians, on the other hand, did not ask me that.'

9. Apollonius lay under one of the trees, and answered any questions his disciples put to him, while Damis took Timasion aside and asked him privately, 'You have met these Naked Philosophers, I suppose, my friend: what are the subjects of their knowledge?'

'There are many important subjects,' he replied.

'Still, it is not wise of them, sir,' said Damis, 'to act like this with us. Refusing to converse with a man like this one about philosophy and putting on airs with him are things I can only describe as insolence, my friend.'

'Insolence?' said Timasion. 'That is something I have never seen in them, though I have been here twice before. They have always been courteous and kind to visitors. Why, not long ago, two months back perhaps, there was a Thrasybulus staying here, a man without any distinction in philosophy, and yet they greeted him warmly, because he called himself a follower of Euphrates.'

'What did you say, young man?' asked Damis. 'Did you see Thrasybulus of Naucratis in the community here?'

'Not only that,' said the boy, 'but I took him in my own boat when he was returning from here.'

'I see it all, for heaven's sake,' said Damis, with a shout of indignation; 'there has been a trick, it seems.'

Timasion replied, 'When I asked the master's name yesterday, he did not let me into the secret; so tell me who it is, if you are not sworn to silence. I might be able to help you in finding what you are looking for.' When he was told by Damis that it was the man from Tyana, he said, 'You were right. When Thrasybulus was sailing down the Nile with me, I asked him why he had come up here, and he described a dishonourable trick of his. He was claiming he had made the Naked Philosophers full of suspicion about Apollonius so that he would be disregarded when he arrived. Why he is an enemy of his I don't know, but to resort to slander seems to me womanish and ignorant. I could find out their attitude by talking to them, because they are friends of mine.'

Timasion came back at evening, and said nothing to Apollonius, except that he had talked to them, but reported to Damis privately that they would be coming the next day, filled with Thrasybulus's stories.

10. That evening they had an ordinary discussion not worth recording, and lay down to sleep where they had eaten. The next day Apollonius was absorbed in contemplation of something, after worshipping the sun in his usual way, when Nilus, the youngest of the Naked Philosophers, ran up to him and said, 'We are coming to you.'

'That is reasonable,' said Apollonius, 'since I came to you here all the way from the sea,' and with these words followed Nilus. He and the philosophers met by the colonnade, and after he had greeted them and received a greeting in return, he said, 'Where shall we talk?'

'Here,' said Thespesion, pointing to the grove. This Thespesion was the senior among the Naked Philosophers, and he walked at their head while they followed him at a dignified and leisurely pace, like Judges of the Hellenes behind the chief Judge. Then they sat down anywhere, abandoning their order, and all looked at Thespesion as the chairman of the discussion. He began in this way:

'I am told that you have visited Delphi and Olympia, Apollonius, since that is what was reported here by Stratocles of Pharos, who said he had met you there. I believe also that Delphi greets its visitors with pipes, songs and lyre-music, and treats them to comedy and tragedy, and only after all this provides the naked competition: Olympia, however, avoids such preliminaries as unbecoming and improper there, and entertains its visitors to the sight of naked athletes according to the arrangements made by Hercules. That is how you must consider our life compared with the philosophy of the Indians. They beguile you with a variety of enchantments, as if they were inviting you to Delphi, but we are naked, as if we were at Olympia. Here the earth does not provide bedding or produce milk or wine as it does to followers of Bacchus, and the air does not hold us suspended. We make the earth itself our bed, and live off its material products, so that it may supply them willingly and not be tortured against its will. However, to show that we have the power to work miracles,' he spoke to a certain tree, an elm which was third in the row from the one under which they were conversing, and said to it, 'Speak to the wise Apollonius.' The tree spoke to him as it was told, and its voice was articulate and feminine.

He made these remarks about the Indians in the belief that he would convert Apollonius from his regard for them, because Apollonius told everybody about the words and the deeds of the Indians. Thespesion added that it was enough for a wise man to keep himself undefiled by the flesh of living things, by the desire that enters through the eyes, and by jealousy which visits hands and hearts to teach them evil, and that truth did not need miracles and magic arts.

'Look at Apollo of Delphi,' he said. 'He dwells in the middle of Greece to dispense oracles. As you know yourself, anybody needing the god's advice asks a brief question, and Apollo tells all he knows without any miracles. It would be easy for him to shake all of Parnassus, to change the waters of Castalia and make them wine, or to stop the Cephisus from being a river. But Apollo reveals the simple truth without any such flourish. We should not think that he even wants to receive the gold or the dedications that we think so fine, or that he prides himself on his temple, nor would he even if it were to be made twice the size it now is. This god once lived in a humble cottage; a little hut was made for him to which the bees contributed wax and the birds their feathers. Thrift is the teacher of wisdom, as it is of truth, and if you follow it you will be considered entirely wise, and will forget the stories you heard from the Indians. "Do this" or "don't do this", "I know" or "I don't know", "this but not that" do not need pomp or storms, or rather brainstorms.

'You have seen in descriptions or pictures the Hercules of Prodicus. Hercules is a youth and has not yet chosen a way of life, and Vice and Virtue both take hold of him and try to draw him to their side. Vice is adorned in gold, ornaments, purple robes; her face is made up, her hair coiffured, and her eyes pencilled; and she has golden shoes, since she is shown flaunting these too. Virtue, however, looks like a woman used to work, with a frowning expression, with wrinkles instead of cosmetics, with bare feet and squalid clothing, and in fact she would appear naked except that she observes the feminine proprieties. Well, Apollonius, think of yourself standing between the wisdom of India and Egypt. You can hear the Indian kind saying it will strew flowers for you when you go to sleep, give you milk to drink, for heaven's sake, and honey to eat: you will have nectar and wines whenever you like; it will wheel in tripods and golden thrones for you when you drink, and you will have no work; everything will come of its own accord. But you can hear Egyptian philosophy saying that it's your duty to sleep on the bare ground, to be seen working naked, like us, not to think anything welcome or pleasant unless it is the fruit of your labour, not to boast or to be fond of vanity, and even to avoid visions that lift you from the earth. If you were to choose like Hercules, showing an iron will and not disregarding the truth or shunning a humble life according to nature, you will be able to say that you have captured many lions and exterminated many hydras, Geryons and Nessuses, and all the creatures that fell before Hercules. If you choose the life of those parasites, however, you will be indulging your eyes and ears, you will be thought no better than anyone else, and you will turn out to have fallen before a Naked Philosopher of Egypt.'

11. When he had spoken, the company turned towards Apollonius. His followers knew that he would answer, but Thespesion's party wondered what he could say. Apollonius praised Thespesion for his fluency and power, and said, 'Do you have anything to add?'

'Of course not,' he said, 'I have finished.'

'Does any of the other Egyptians?' asked Apollonius.

'You heard them all,' replied Thespesion, 'when you heard me.'

Apollonius then was silent for a little while, with his attention concentrated on what Thespesion had said; and then he began, 'Your account, Wise Men of Egypt, of Hercules's choice, which according to Prodicus he made as a young man, was wise and true to the spirit of philosophy, but it has nothing to do with me. I have not come here to take your advice about a way of life, since I long ago chose the one that seemed right to me. I am also older than all of you except Thespesion, so that I, your visitor, would have been better suited to advise you about choosing a philosophy, except that I find you have already chosen one.

'However, old as I am, and far advanced in wisdom, I will not hesitate to let you inspect my choice, and will show you how right I was to choose my path, since I have never observed a better one. I saw a sign of greatness in Pythagoras. His mysterious philosophy not only enabled him to know his own true self but also his past identity; he approached altars in purity, he kept his stomach undefiled by the flesh of living things, and his body uncontaminated by all clothes made from dead creatures; he was the first man to hold his tongue by inventing "the ox on the tongue" as a rule of silence;[6] the rest of his philosophy was oracular and true. I therefore ran to embrace his doctrines. I did not choose one philosophy out of two, as you advise, Thespesion. Philosophy set the whole variety of her doctrines before me, adorning each with its own special charms, and then told me to look at them and choose wisely. All of them had a venerable, divine beauty, and some were such as to make other men dazzled with amazement. I, however, looked steadily at them all, as they themselves encouraged me to do, by trying to win me over and by promising all the things they would give me. This one said that without any toil I would taste a great feast of pleasures;[7] that one, that I would toil and then rest;[8] another, that she would mix delights with toil,[9] and on every side I could see pleasures, all restraints on gluttony abandoned, hands grasping for wealth, the eyes unblinkered; love, desire and all such experiences were permitted. Another philosophy boasted that she would restrain me from such things:[10] she was rude, quarrelsome, and contemptuous of everything. But I saw a mysterious kind of philosophy, which once won the devotion of

6. An ox on one's tongue was a proverbial allusion to keeping silent. cf., for example, Aeschylus, *Agamemnon*, 36.

7. Epicureanism.

8. Stoicism.   9. Peripateticism.

10. Cynicism.

Pythagoras. She was not standing in the crowd, but apart from them and in silence. Seeing that I resisted the others, but did not yet know her own gifts, she said, "Young man, I have no pleasures, and am full of labour. A man who joins my society must choose to put aside all food that consists of living flesh: he must forget wine, and not cloud the vessel of wisdom that stands in the hearts of those that drink no wine. No cloak or wool shorn from a living creature shall warm him, and I give him shoes of bark and the ground he stands on as a bed. If I see him yield to sex, I have abysses to which justice, the servant of wisdom, takes him and pushes him down. So harsh am I to those that choose my way that I have bits to curb their tongues. But let me tell you what the reward is if you endure all this. You will of course be self-controlled and just: you will need to envy no one: you will terrify tyrants rather than be in their power: you will please the gods more with humble sacrifices than those who spill the blood of bulls for them, and being pure you will receive from me the gift of foreknowledge, and I will so fill your eyes with radiance that you will recognize gods, know heroes, and unmask insubstantial ghosts when they hide in mortal form."

'This is the way of life I have chosen, Egyptian philosophers. I chose it honestly and by Pythagoras's example, and I neither deceived myself nor was deceived, because I have become what a philosopher should become, and I have been given all that my philosophy said it would give me if I did. My philosophy has been concerned with the being and the origins of the art: and I have observed that it belongs to men who are expert in divine science and have the truest conception of the soul, because it is the soul, subject neither to death nor to birth, that is the source of being.'

12. Damis says that when he heard this, he breathed again, since Apollonius's words had such an effect on the Egyptians

that Thespesion could be clearly seen blushing, black though he was. The others too showed amazement at Apollonius's conviction and eloquence, and the youngest of the Egyptians, who was named Nilus, apparently jumped up in admiration, and going over to Apollonius gave him his hand and asked him to tell about the conversation he had had with the Indians.

Apollonius replied, 'I would have no objection to telling you anything, because I can see you are willing to listen and are friendly to every kind of philosophy, but I would not care to burden Thespesion with talk of the Indians, or anybody else who considers their wisdom nonsense.'

Thespesion then said, 'Suppose you were a merchant or a captain bringing some cargo to us from there. Would you expect to dispose of it without submitting it to examination, just because it was from India, and not allow it to be tested or seen?'

'If anybody wanted,' replied Apollonius, 'I would let them inspect it. But suppose somebody came down to the shore when my boat had just put in, and denounced my cargo, accusing it of coming from a land that produced nothing good; and suppose he attacked me for trading in debased goods, and persuaded everyone else to believe him. Do you imagine that someone who had sailed into such a harbour would let out his anchor or cable at all? Wouldn't he rather hoist his sails and put out again to the open sea, and trust his goods to the breezes rather than to undiscriminating and un-friendly people?'

'Well,' said Nilus, 'I grasp the cables and beg you, captain, to give me some of the cargo you have. I would be willing to come on your ship as a deck-hand and look after the cargo.'

13. Thespesion, wanting to cut this talk short, said, 'I am glad,

Apollonius, that what you have heard annoys you. You will be all the readier to pardon us for being annoyed at the way you criticized our philosophy when you had not yet come to test it.'

For a moment, Apollonius was taken aback by these words, not yet having heard the story about Thrasybulus and Euphrates. Then, seeing what had happened, as he usually did, he said, 'No, Thespesion, the Indians would have reacted differently. They would not have listened to Euphrates when he put this story about, because they have the gift of fore-knowledge. My quarrel with Euphrates was not about any personal matter. I tried to wean him from moneymaking and from being satisfied with profit wherever it came from. But it seems that my advice was inappropriate and beyond his power. He thinks it was condemnation, and never stops devising some new plot against me.

'You believed him when he slandered my character, but you must remember that he slandered you rather than me. It seems to me that a man who is destined to incur slander will run into no small danger and be hated when he has done no harm: but those who listen to slander will be proved to esteem falsehood and to put as high a value on it as on truth; second, they will be convicted of silliness and gullibility, which it is disgraceful even for a boy to succumb to; they will be considered jealous, because they allow their jealousy to give them prejudiced information, and to be more guilty themselves of the slanders which they believe true when they hear them from others: human nature is all the more inclined to do what it does not refuse to believe about other people. May a man ready to do this never be a tyrant, or a popular leader either, because democracy will become tyranny in his hands; may he not be a judge, because he will not judge in favour of either party, nor a ship's captain, because the crew will quarrel, or lead an army, because the enemy will profit, or be a philosopher with such a nature, because he will not judge according to the truth. Euphrates has deprived you of your wisdom, because no one that he has misled by his lies can think themselves worthy of wisdom; they have been seduced from it by the man who persuaded them of something incredible.'

To mollify him, Thespesion said, 'Enough of Euphrates and narrow-minded topics. We would be glad to reconcile the two of you, because we think it the philosopher's duty to settle philosophers' disputes.'

'But who will reconcile me with you?' asked Apollonius. 'Since I have been falsely slandered, I ought to be your enemy because of the falsehood. But let us leave it there, and start a discussion: that will reconcile us sooner.'

14. Nilus, full of eagerness to listen to Apollonius, said, 'Well, it is you that should begin the conversation by telling us about your journey to the country of the Indians and your conversations there. They must have been on exalted subjects.'

'For my part,' said Thespesion, 'I am keen to hear about the wisdom of Phraotes, since I am told you have brought from India precious extracts from his conversation.' Apollonius therefore began with their experiences in Babylon, and described their whole story, while the Egyptians were delighted to listen, and hung on his words. When noon came, they ended their conversation, since this is a time which the Naked Philosophers as well devote to religion.

15. When Apollonius and his company were at dinner, Nilus came bringing vegetables, bread and fruits, some of which he carried himself while the rest were carried by others. With great friendliness he said, 'The wise men send these as gifts

to you and me. I am going to dine with you, not uninvited, as the saying is, but invited by myself.'

'It is a welcome gift you bring,' said Apollonius, 'in your-self and your virtue, young man. You seem to be a genuine philosopher, and well disposed to the doctrines of the Indians and of Pythagoras. Sit down here and join our company.'

'I will sit down,' he said, 'but you do not have enough food to satisfy me.'

'You seem to have a good appetite and to be fond of eating,' said Apollonius.

'Extremely fond,' was the reply. 'Despite the great, brilliant feast you have spread, I am still not full, and after a short while I have come to eat again. You cannot call me anything but an insatiable, terrible glutton.'

'Eat your fill,' said Apollonius, 'but the food for argument at any rate you must provide yourself, and I will provide the rest.'

16. When they had dined, Nilus said, 'Up to now I have campaigned with the Naked Philosophers, and made common cause with them as if they used light armour or slings; but now I carry heavy arms and your shield will be my glory.'

'I am afraid, my Egyptian friend,' said Apollonius, 'that Thespesion and the others will blame you because, without testing us any further, you have joined our society more readily than choosing a way of life usually permits.'

'Perhaps so,' said Nilus, 'but if choosing involves blame, failure to choose perhaps does too, so that they will be more to blame if they choose the course that I have chosen. They are older and wiser too, and their failure to make long ago the choice that I am making now might be good grounds for blaming them, since with their greater advantages they have not made a better choice of the way to follow.'

'These are excellent words, young man,' said Apollonius,

'but simply because those philosophers are so advanced in wisdom and in age, they may in fact prove to be right in choosing their way and correct in refusing ours: and you may prove to have spoken rather rashly in trying to set them right yourself instead of listening to them.'

The Egyptian, correcting the supposition of Apollonius, said, 'I have not failed to obey them in every way that a young man might reasonably obey his elders. As long as I thought they had wisdom such as belonged to no other men, I made myself their disciple. The reason for my decision was this. My father once sailed to the Red Sea of his own free will,[11] since he was captain of the ship which the Egyptians sent to India. He conversed with the Indians of the shore, and brought back stories about the wise men there similar to those you recounted to us. I also heard from him some such story as this, that the Indians were the wisest men of all, but that the Ethiopians were migrants from India and maintained their ancestral wisdom and observed their original traditions. When I grew up, therefore, I gave my inheritance to whoever wanted it and joined these Naked Philosophers as naked as they were, hoping to learn Indian lore or something like it. The Naked Philosophers seemed wise to me, but not in the lore of India, and when I asked them why their philosophy was not of the Indian kind, they started to slander the Indians rather in the way they did to you today. And they enrolled me in their community when I was still young, as you see, I suppose because they were afraid I would turn my back on them and sail off to the Red Sea as my father once did. That indeed I would have done, and in fact I would have gone as far as the wise men's hill if some god had not sent you here to help me. In this way, without sailing to the Red Sea or putting in among the Bay-Dwellers, I was to taste Indian philosophy; I

11. See the note on III. 20 above for what was meant by 'Red Sea' in antiquity.

was not waiting to choose my way of life today, since I made that choice long ago, even if I did not obtain what I thought I would.

'What is so surprising if someone resumes his former pursuit when he missed his object before? If I tried to bring them over to this path and advised them to believe what I am convinced is true, would that be arrogant of me, do you think? Youth must not be denied the power of reaching some better conclusions than old age, and anybody who urges someone else to adopt a philosophy he has chosen himself is certainly not liable to the charge of preaching what he does not believe. When chance brings blessings, the person who seizes them solely for his own enjoyment is abusing them by denying them an opportunity to bring greater pleasure to others.'

17. When Nilus had finished pouring out these youthful ideas, Apollonius replied, 'Well, aren't you going to agree with me on a fee, if you are attracted by my philosophy?'

'Let us agree,' said Nilus, 'and ask for what you want.'

'I ask this: that you persevere in your choice, but not bother the Naked Philosophers by giving advice that will not be accepted.'

'I will agree to that,' said Nilus, 'and let this be the fee.'

This was the end of their discussion. Afterwards Nilus asked Apollonius how long he would stay with the Naked Philosophers, and he replied, 'As long as their wisdom repays a man for their company. Then we will travel to the Cataracts to see the source of the Nile. It would be pleasant not only to see the headwaters of the river, but to hear it roaring.' After this conversation, and discussion of certain Indian matters, they went to sleep on the grass.

. . . . .

23. At dawn the next day, after saying goodbye to the Naked Philosophers, they started on the road that leads to the mountains, with the Nile on their right, and saw the following notable sights. The Mountains of the Cataracts are earthy and about the size of the Tmolus in Lydia. The Nile flows down from them, and the soil it carries becomes the land of Egypt. The noise of the stream as it falls from the mountain and crashes down into the Nile is apparently overwhelming and unbearable to the ears: many people have come too close and returned without their sense of hearing.

24. As Apollonius and his party advanced, they could see conical mountains with trees growing on them of which the leaves, the bark and the gum are gathered by the Egyptians. Near the road they saw lions, leopards and other such animals: none of these approached them, but all fled as if terrified of human beings. They also observed deer, gazelles, ostriches and asses, all of them in large numbers, but even larger numbers of wild bulls and goat-oxen, creatures that are respectively a cross between a deer and a bull and between the two animals from which their name comes. Of these they also saw bones and half-eaten carcasses, because lions satisfy their hunger when the victim is still warm and neglect the remaining parts, I suppose because they are sure of catching more.

25. In that region also live the nomad Ethiopians in caravan communities, and next to them, the elephant hunters: these cut up their quarry and sell it, and so have a name which refers to their selling elephant meat. Nasamones, Cannibals, Pygmies and Shadowfooted Men are other Ethiopian tribes, and reach as far as the Ethiopian Ocean, into which nobody sails except when carried off course accidentally.

26. The company was conversing about these animals and speculating about nature and the different way it feeds different creatures, when they heard a noise like that of thunder when it is not yet overpowering but still muffled inside the cloud. 'The cataract is near, gentlemen,' said Timasion, 'the last as you go down river but the first as you go up.' After proceeding about a mile and a quarter they apparently saw a river breaking from the mountainside which was no less in quantity than the Marsyas and Maeander where they first join. After praying to the Nile, they went on, but no longer saw animals, because these dislike noise and prefer silent haunts to noisy, reverberating ones. After about two miles they heard another cataract, this time overwhelming and impossible to listen to, since it was twice the volume of the previous one and fell from higher mountains. Damis says that he and another member of the company were so deafened that he himself turned back and begged Apollonius not to go on. Apollonius, however, went on confidently with Timasion and Nilus to the third cataract, and reported the following when he came back: crags about a mile high overhang the Nile there, and the bank that faces the mountains is a cliff of strangely shaped stone. The water as it cascades from the mountains falls on to the rocky bank, and from there pours into the Nile white and frothing. The effects caused by these falls, which are much greater than the previous ones, and by the noise that echoes from them to the mountains apparently makes investigation of the stream dangerous to the hearing. The road leading on to the very source, it seems, is impossible to travel or even to imagine, because there are many poetic stories about spirits there, such as Pindar's masterly poem about the spirit which he represents as guarding this source to ensure the regular flow of the Nile.[12]

12. Pindar's poem has not survived.

27. After the cataracts, they stopped in a not very large village of Ethiopia, and were having their evening dinner, mixing light and serious topics, when they heard a sudden shout from the women in the village. They were encouraging each other to 'catch and chase it', and also calling in their husbands to help with the task; the men grabbed clubs, stones and anything that came to hand and were shouting for their friends as if they had caught an adulterer. It emerged that for nine months the village had been visited by the apparition of a satyr, which was mad for women and was already said to have killed the two it apparently desired most. The company was terrified, but Apollonius said, 'Don't be afraid. There is a satyr loose here.'

'There certainly is,' said Nilus. 'It has been loose here for some time now, and we Naked Philosophers have never yet induced it to stop its frolics.'

'There is a remedy for these nuisances,' said Apollonius, 'which Midas is said to have used once.[13] He himself was related to the satyrs, as his ears showed; and there was a satyr who took advantage of his relationship to insult Midas by making fun of his ears, not only by singing but also by piping about them. Now Midas had heard, from his mother I suppose, that if a satyr is overcome by wine and falls asleep, it will behave and become friendly. So he mixed wine into the fountain near his palace and let the satyr use it, so that the creature drank and was caught. To prove that the story is true, let us go to the head of the village, and if the villagers have wine, let us mix some for the satyr, and it will have the same effect on him as on Midas's one.'

They agreed to this, and Apollonius poured four Egyptian jars of wine into a trough from which the village herds drank. Then he summoned the satyr, reproaching it in some mysteri-

13. Midas was a legendary king of Phrygia, famed for possessing fabulous wealth and the ears of an ass.

ous way; and without the creature being seen the wine began to go down as if someone was drinking. When it had all been drunk, Apollonius said, 'Let us make a truce with the satyr, since he is asleep.' So saying, he led the villagers to a cave of the Nymphs, not quite a hundred feet from the village, in which he showed them the satyr sleeping, and told them to refrain from hitting or scolding it, because it had stopped its silly tricks.

So much for the deed of Apollonius, certainly not 'a passing errand on the journey' but an errand on the passing journey. If you read a letter of his written to a misbehaved youth in which he claims to have given a lesson to a supernatural satyr in Ethiopia, you ought to recall this story.

That satyrs exist and have love-affairs is something that should be believed. I know of a contemporary of mine in Lemnos[14] whose mother was said to be visited by what appears from the present story to have been a satyr: he appeared to wear a close-fitting coat of fawnskin on his back, with the forefeet drawn around his neck and tied over his chest. That is enough of this subject, however, because there is no reason to disbelieve either the evidence of the senses or myself.

28. When Apollonius had returned from Ethiopia, his quarrel with Euphrates developed more and more because of their daily discussions, but Apollonius left these to Menippus and Nilus. He himself only rebuked Euphrates a little, since he was spending a lot of time with Nilus.

29. Titus had now taken Jerusalem with enormous slaughter,[15] and the neighbouring lands were sending him crowns. Titus,

14. Philostratus and his family were natives of the island of Lemnos in the Aegean.

15. Jerusalem fell in August A.D. 70.

however, did not think he deserved them, because he had not accomplished all this himself but had only lent his help when heaven showed its anger. Apollonius approved of this: Titus seemed to him to have sense and an understanding of the ways of gods and men, and it seemed a sign of great self-control not to want a crown for bloodshed. So Apollonius wrote a letter to him and sent Damis to carry it. It ran as follows:

'Apollonius greets Titus, the general of the Romans.

'Though you did not want to be proclaimed the victor with the spear or in the slaughter of war, I give you the crown for self-control, because you know what deeds deserve a crown. Good-bye.'

Titus was delighted with this letter, and replied, 'I thank you on my own behalf and on my father's, and I will remember this. Jerusalem is my prisoner, and I am yours.'

30. When Titus had been declared emperor in Rome and had been judged to deserve this reward, he left to share his father's power.[16] Realizing, however, that Apollonius would be of great service to him even from a short meeting, he asked him to come to Tarsus. When Apollonius arrived Titus embraced him and said, 'My father has written to me about all the subjects on which he asked your advice. Here is his letter. He writes that you are his helper and indeed responsible for our whole position. But I am only thirty: and I have been accorded the status which my father has at sixty, and am being summoned to rule before I am even sure I know how to be ruled; and so I am afraid I am assuming a higher position than I ought.'

Apollonius felt Titus's neck, a part in which he was as strong as a trained athlete, and said, 'Who will force a bull to put such a strong neck beneath the yoke?'

16. Titus was given important constitutional prerogatives such as his father Vespasian had and was thereby marked out as the next emperor.

'The man who trained me from boyhood,' said Titus, meaning his father, and indicating that he would only be governed by the man who had made him accustomed to listen to his voice from boyhood.

'It pleases me,' said Apollonius, 'above all to see you prepared to follow your father, who receives willing submission even from those who are not his own sons, and to see you waiting in attendance on the man with whom you will be waited on yourself. When youth, moreover, joins with age in government, there is a beautiful, concordant harmony to surpass that of any lyre or any pipe. The ways of the old and of the young will be joined together, and will make age strong and youth well behaved.'

31. 'What advice,' asked Titus, 'do you have for me about ruling an empire, man of Tyana?'

'Advice of which you are already convinced,' said Apollonius, 'because as your father's follower you will obviously come to resemble him. I would also at this point mention the words of Archytas, because they are excellent and worth remembering. Archytas was a man of Tarentum, wise in the doctrine of Pythagoras; and in a work on the education of children he says, "Let the father be a lesson in virtue to his children. Fathers will be all the keener to attain the virtues if their own sons come to resemble them." I will also introduce my friend Demetrius to you, and he will converse with you on any subject you want, teaching you how a good ruler should behave.'

'What kind of philosophy,' asked Titus, 'does this man practise, Apollonius?'

'Frankness,' he replied, 'truth, and complete fearlessness, since he is of the Cynic persuasion.'

Titus was not pleased to hear the word 'Cynic', and Apollonius continued, 'Because Telemachus was young, Homer thought he needed two dogs, and he sends them to accompany the young man to the marketplace of Ithaca, unreasoning animals though they are.[17] You will have a dog that will bark for your good at other people, and at you too if you do any wrong, and it will do so wisely and with reason.'

'Let me have that dog to go with me,' said Titus. 'I even give it permission to bite me, if it sees me doing any wrong.'

'I will write him a letter,' said Apollonius, 'since he practises in Rome.'

'Do so,' Titus replied; 'I only wish someone would write to you for my sake, and make you travel the road to Rome with me.'

'I will come,' said Apollonius, 'when it is best for us both.'

32. Then Titus dismissed those present and said, 'We are alone, man of Tyana. You will allow me, I presume, to question you on the subject most important to me?'

'Do so,' said Apollonius, 'and do so with all the more readiness, as the subject is so important.'

'My question,' said Titus, 'concerns my own life and the people I should most be on guard against. I hope I shall not seem a coward for worrying about the matter already.'

'No,' replied Apollonius, 'you seem cautious and vigilant, because this is something over which you must take the greatest care.' Looking up at the sun, he swore to Titus that he had been intending to advise him on these matters without even being asked; the gods, he said, had ordered him in a vision to warn Titus to fear his father's greatest enemies, while his father lived, and after his death those closest to himself.

'How shall I die?' asked Titus.

'The way Odysseus is supposed to have died,' said Apol-

17. Apollonius is playing with the meaning of the Greek word Cynic, which is correlative with the word for dog. The Homeric reference is to *Odyssey* II. 11.

lonius; 'he too, they say, met a death that came from the sea.'

This remark Damis expounds as follows. Titus took pre-cautions against the sting of the sting-ray, by which Odysseus is supposed to have been killed, but when he had been em-peror for two years after his father's death he was killed by means of a sea-hare. This fish produces a peculiar liquid, more poisonous than any other creature on land or sea. Nero used to mix this sea-hare into his dishes to dispose of his greatest enemies, and Domitian used it to dispose of his brother Titus, not because he dreaded sharing power with his brother so much as doing so with a kind and honest man.[18]

After this conversation in private, they embraced publicly; and as Titus left, Apollonius said, 'Surpass your enemies in arms, emperor, and your father in virtues.'

33. His letter to Demetrius, however, ran like this:

'Apollonius the philosopher greets Demetrius the Cynic:

'I have provided the emperor Titus with you as his teacher in the conduct of his rule. Please do me the favour of speaking truth to him, and give him all your qualities except your anger. Good-bye.'

34. The inhabitants of Tarsus had previously disliked Apol-lonius because of the severity of his rebukes, and because their own laxity and extravagance made them unable to bear firmness even in language. On this occasion, however, they were so won over by him as to consider him the founder and the mainstay of the city. The emperor was making a public sacrifice, when the citizens assembled together to make a very urgent petition to him. Titus replied that he would mention it to his father and convey their request personally. Apollonius came up to him and said, 'Suppose I were to show that some

18. It was suspected that Domitian caused Titus's death: cf. Suetonius *Domitian* 2. 3 and Cassius Dio LXVI. 26.

of these people were enemies of you and your father, that they had negotiated with Jerusalem on the subject of rebellion and had been secretly allied to your most obvious enemy. What would happen to them?'

'They would be exterminated, of course,' said Titus.

'Well then,' replied Apollonius, 'isn't it disgraceful to expect revenge immediately, but to grant benefactions slowly? To make yourself responsible for the first, and to refer the second to deliberations with others?'

The emperor was delighted, and said, 'I grant the gifts; my father will not be angry with me for giving in to truth and to you.'

35. These are the countries that Apollonius is said to have travelled till then, conversing and becoming the subject of conversation. His travels thereafter were many, though they were not so numerous as before, and did not involve countries other than the ones he knew. He had had a long stay in the coastal region of Egypt when he returned from Ethiopia, and similarly in Phoenicia, Cilicia, Ionia, Achaea and Italy, never failing wherever he was to seem the same as before. To know yourself is considered difficult: but more difficult, it seems to me, is for a wise man to remain true to himself, since he cannot change evil natures for the better unless he has first trained himself not to change. This is a subject on which I have written at length in another work;[19] in this I teach those who study it rigorously that a true man will neither change nor become a slave. But I do not want to go to great lengths by relating in detail Apollonius's philosophical activity in every place, or on the other hand to appear to skimp the account which I am composing, not without trouble to myself, for the benefit of those who do not know about Apollonius. I think it best, therefore, to recount the more important discourses

19. This other work of Philostratus cannot be identified.

and such as seem worth noting. They should be considered as valuable as the visits of Asclepius's servants.

36. There was a young man who despite his own lack of education taught birds and kept them to make them clever. He had trained them to say everything that humans can, and to make every tune that pipes can. When Apollonius met him, he said, 'What is your profession?' The young man described his nightingales and blackbirds and all the words he was teaching to his plovers, though he himself spoke in an obviously uneducated way. Apollonius said to him, 'You seem to me to be spoiling your birds, above all by not letting them use their own voices, which are so sweet that even musical instruments are unable to imitate them; and second, by teaching them incomprehensibility, since you talk the worst possible Greek yourself.

'Besides, young man, you are also wasting your fortune. When I look at your servants and your appearance, I have the impression that you are extravagant and reasonably wealthy, and people such as you are sucked dry by parasites, who use their tongues to spur you on. What use will your bird-fancying be then? Even if you use all your nightingales' songs, you won't be able to scare those parasites off when they press you and harry you; you will have to unload all your property and throw money to them like scraps to angry dogs, and if they bark, to give them more and more; then you yourself will go hungry and poor later. You need some honourable escape, some immediate change in your ways. Otherwise you may find you have shed all your wealth, and that you deserve to be mourned by birds rather than serenaded.

'The remedy to change you is nothing special. There is a breed of men in every city whom you do not yet know, but they are called teachers. Give them a little of your property, and you will enjoy the remainder in security, because they will teach you the simple art of public speaking. If I saw that you were still a boy, I would advise you to attend philosophers and sophists and fortify your own house with every kind of wisdom. But you are too old for that now, so at least learn to speak in your own interest. Remember that if your education had been thorough, you would seem like a man heavily armed and formidable: but if you have this education, you will receive the equipment of a light-armed soldier and a sling-fighter, because you will be able to hit parasites as one hits dogs.'

The young man took this to heart, left his hobby of bird-training and attended teachers. As a result both his mind and his tongue improved.

37. Apollonius heard two stories in Sardis, one being that the Pactolus River once carried gold-dust, to the profit of Croesus, and the other that trees were older than the earth. The first he said was rightly believed, since the Tmolus had once contained powdered gold which the rain had washed away into the Pactolus; but in time as often happened the gold had become exhausted and disappeared. But he laughed at the other story, saying, 'You claim that trees existed before the earth. But in all the time I have been a philosopher I have never heard that the stars existed before the sky.' By this he conveyed that nothing could come into existence without whatever contained it already existing.

38. The governor of Syria was causing dissension in Antioch, and sowing suspicion among the inhabitants, so as to cause a rift among the citizens during a public meeting. Just then a serious earthquake occurred which made them cower and pray for each other, as usually happens in upheavals of nature. Apollonius came forward and said, 'God has clearly shown himself your mediator. You should not quarrel again for fear

of the same thing.' Thus the citizens realized what would happen to them, and that both factions would have the same thing to fear.

. . . . .

41. The cities on the left side of the Hellespont were once shaken by earthquakes. Egyptians and Chaldaeans went begging from one to the other to collect money for a sacrifice of ten talents that they said they were going to make to Earth and Poseidon. The cities began to make contributions partly from their treasuries and partly from private possessions, since they were in the grip of fear. But the beggars said that they would not sacrifice unless the money were paid cash down. Apollonius decided not to overlook the plight of the Hellespontines, and visited the cities, driving out the visitors for profiteering in this way from the misfortunes of others. Then, realizing the causes of the gods' anger, he made the sacrifice appropriate to each city, and so obtained deliverance from the disaster at a small cost, and the earth stopped moving.

42. The emperor Domitian made two laws about the same time, that males were not to be castrated and vines not to be planted, and moreover vines that had been were to be cut down.[20] Apollonius came before the Ionians and said, 'These edicts do not concern me, because I am perhaps the only human being not to need either genitals or wine. But this extraordinary man does not realize that he is sparing men while castrating the earth.' That gave Ionia the courage to send an embassy to the emperor about vines, and to request the

20. Suetonius mentions both the emperor's edict against castration (*Domitian* 7. 1) and the vine edict (*Domitian* 14. 2). The vine edict is dated by Eusebius to A.D. 91/2, and it is alluded to by the contemporary poet, Statius, in a poem datable to A.D. 95 (*Silvae* IV. 3. 11–12). Philostratus later mentioned the vine edict again in his biography of the sophist Scopelian (Book I of the *Lives of the Sophists*).

repeal of a law which made it mandatory both to ravage the earth and not to plant it.

43. There is another celebrated story about Apollonius in Tarsus. A mad dog attacked a young man in such a way that the bite had made the boy behave just like a dog: he barked, howled, and ran on all fours with his hands on the ground. He had been ill for thirty days when Apollonius, who had just arrived in Tarsus, ordered the discovery of the dog responsible for all this. They said that they had never seen the creature, since the young man had been bitten outside the wall when practising with the javelin, and it was impossible to find out from the victim what the dog looked like, since he did not even recognize himself. After a pause, Apollonius said, 'Damis, it is a white, shaggy sheep-dog, the size of the Amphilochian kind, and it is standing by such-and-such a fountain' (which he named) 'trembling because it both desires and fears water. Bring it to me by the river bank where the wrestling grounds are. You need only say that Apollonius is summoning it.' When Damis had dragged the dog along, it lay at Apollonius's feet, groaning like a suppliant at an altar; and Apollonius made it even tamer by stroking it with his hand. He then made the boy stand nearby, bringing him close so that the crowd could see a great miracle, and then said, 'The soul of Telephus the Mysian has entered this boy,[21] and the Fates require the same treatment for him.' So saying, he told the dog to lick the bite, so that the boy's wounder should also be his healer. Immediately the boy turned to greet his father, recognized his mother, spoke to his friends, and took a drink from the Cydnus. Apollonius did not neglect the dog, but after a prayer to the river told the creature to swim across.

21. Telephus, a king of Mysia, was wounded by Achilles. An oracle declared that the wounder should be the healer, and Telephus was healed by the rust of Achilles's spear.

When it had crossed the Cydnus, it stood on the bank and barked, which does not happen at all when dogs are rabid; and it bent back its ears and wagged its tail, in the knowledge that it had been cured, since water is the medicine for rabies if the victim has the courage to drink it.

These are the actions of Apollonius on behalf of sanctuaries and cities, his speeches to populaces and on their behalf, his help to the dead and the sick, and his conversation with the wise, the ignorant, and those emperors that asked his advice about virtue.

BOOK VII

1. I am aware that tyranny is the surest test of philosophers, and I am not opposed to studying the respects in which each of them has proved more or less resolute than another. This is my introduction to what follows.

In the days when Domitian was tyrant, Apollonius was beset by accusations and indictments. Their causes, agents, and their precise terms I will discuss soon. It is my duty to record what it was that Apollonius said and what he revealed himself to be that caused him to leave court after condemning the tyrant rather than be condemned himself. Before this, however, I have decided to recount all the noteworthy deeds I have been able to find performed by wise men in the face of tyranny, and to compare them to those of Apollonius, because this is how we must discover truth.

2. Zeno of Elea, the reputed founder of dialectic, was caught trying to overthrow the tyranny of Nearchus the Mysian.[1] Under torture he made no mention of his fellow conspirators, but accused the tyrant's loyal supporters of being disloyal. These were therefore put to death as if the charges were true, while Zeno led Mysia into freedom by making the tyranny ruin itself.

Plato claims to have joined the struggle for the freedom of Sicily with Dion as his partner in the plan.[2]

1. Zeno of Elea was a philosopher of the fifth century B.C.; he was a pupil of Parmenides.
2. Dion, a relative of Dionysius I of Sicily, attempted under the influence of Plato to direct the policies of the youthful Dionysius II. He failed and subsequently launched an attack on Dionysius.

Phyton was expelled from Rhegium and was given protection by Dionysius the tyrant of Sicily.[3] There he was more highly honoured than is usual for an exile, and realized the king's plan and his designs on Rhegium. He was caught writing to Rhegium about this, and the tyrant had him tied still alive to one of the siege engines which he brought against the walls in the expectation that the inhabitants would spare Phyton rather than fire at the machine. Phyton, however, shouted to them to fire, saying that he was the target of their freedom.

Heraclides and Python, the assassins of Cotys of Thrace, were both young men who chose to study at the Academy and, after becoming wise, they became free.[4]

The story of Callisthenes of Olynthus is generally known.[5] In one and the same day he praised, then criticized the Macedonians when they were at the height of their power, so that they found him displeasing and took his life.

As for Diogenes of Sinope and Crates of Thebes, Diogenes went straight to Chaeronea and reproached Philip because of the Athenians; Philip claimed to be a Heraclid, he charged, and yet he was using arms to destroy the people who had taken up arms to defend the Heraclids.[6] Crates, when Alexander promised to rebuild Thebes for his sake, said that he had no need of a city that someone could destroy by force of arms.[7]

I could recount many such stories, but my work does not

3. Phyton led the resistance of Rhegium in Sicily against Dionysius I, who conquered it in 387 B.C.

4. Heraclides and Python were Thracian brothers who killed, for personal reasons, Cotys I, king of the Odrysian Thracians, in 360/59 B.C.

5. Callisthenes of Olynthus was Aristotle's nephew. He travelled with Alexander the Great and wrote a history of his expedition. He and Alexander quarrelled in 327 B.C.

6. Diogenes of Sinope founded the Cynic school of philosophy. In 338 B.C. Philip II of Macedon decisively defeated the Greeks at Chaeronea in Boeotia.

7. Crates was Diogenes's pupil. In 335 B.C. Alexander utterly destroyed Thebes in Boeotia, sparing only the house of the poet Pindar.

allow me to expand on them, especially since I am obliged to criticize these acts, not on the ground that they are not honourable or widely regarded, but because they are inferior compared with those of Apollonius, even if superior compared with those of anyone else.

3. The deed of the man from Elea and the murder of Cotys are not particularly noteworthy, since it is easy to enslave the Thracians and Goths, and pointless to free them; they do not enjoy liberty, I suppose since they do not consider servitude a disgrace.

I will not claim that Plato did not behave like a wise man in trying to correct the situation in Sicily rather than that at Athens, or that he was rightly sold because of his ruinous effect on himself and others,[8] because that would offend some of my readers.

The man from Rhegium made his plot against Dionysius only when the tyrant was no longer in firm control of Sicily, and he would in any case have been killed by Dionysius if he had not been hit by the inhabitants of Rhegium. I do not think it was a very marvellous achievement to choose death on behalf of other men's freedom, when the alternative was death to save himself from slavery.

Callisthenes cannot escape the imputation of cowardice even now. To make the same people the object of his praise and blame either meant blaming those he thought worthy of praise or praising those he should have openly blamed. Besides, the man who descends to vituperating the upright cannot escape the appearance of malice: and the man who flatters the wicked with praise shares the responsibility for their crimes, because praise makes bad men worse.

8. There was a legend in antiquity that Dionysius I put Plato up for sale at a slave-market in Corinth, where some philosophers were fortunately able to buy him.

If Diogenes had made his remark to Philip before Chaeronea he might have saved him from the disgrace of fighting Athens, but by arriving only when it was over he merely insulted him without any salutary effect. Crates could even be blamed by a patriot for not encouraging Alexander in his proposal to rebuild Thebes.

Apollonius, however, did not tremble because of danger to his native city, or despair of his life, or resort to foolish speeches. His help was not given to Mysians or Goths, his adversary was not the ruler of one island or a small country. It was the lord of the whole earth and sea that Apollonius set himself against for the benefit of the tyrant's subjects when he was ruling harshly. This same course Apollonius had taken with Nero, but that may be considered a mere skirmish, [4] since Apollonius did not come to close quarters, but helped to undermine the tyranny by encouraging Vindex and attacking Tigellinus. On this subject there has grown up the impudent idea that attacking Nero required no courage, because he lived like a woman who plays the harp or the pipe. Nothing like that can be said about Domitian. He was physically strong; he despised the pleasures of musical instruments and drums that weaken vigour; he drew his pleasures from the pains of others and from everything that could cause distress; he called distrust the safeguard of democracy against tyrants and of tyrants against everybody; he thought that night should be the end of an emperor's work and the beginning of his murders; and hence the senate was shorn of its most eminent members, philosophy was so cowed that its followers forgot their roles and some fled to the Celts of the west and others to the deserts of Libya and Scythia, while a few were induced to speak in favour of the emperor's crimes. Not so Apollonius. Sophocles represents Tiresias defending himself before Oedipus with the words, 'I do not live in your service, but Apollo's';[9] and

9. Sophocles, *Oedipus the King*, 410.

similarly, because he had made wisdom his mistress, Apollonius was free from the impulses of Domitian. He applied the words of Tiresias and Sophocles to himself, with the result that he had no fear for himself, but pitied the destruction of others. Thus he turned such courage as the senate retained and such intelligence as he observed in certain of its members into a conspiracy against Domitian, by visiting the provinces and by telling the governors in his discussions that the power of tyrants was not everlasting, and that their very ability to inspire fear made them more vulnerable. He described to them also the Attic Panathenaea, which caused the fame of Harmodius and Aristogeiton, and he described the expedition from Phyle which destroyed all Thirty Tyrants at once,[10] and moreover recounted the ancient history of Rome, and how they had originally been a democracy and had expelled their tyrannies by force.

5. A tragic actor appeared in the play *Ino* at Ephesus, with the governor of Asia in the audience. This man was young and a distinguished consular, but had rather a timid attitude to the prevailing situation. The actor was just finishing the iambic lines in which Euripides says that tyrants need a long time to grow but a small thing to ruin them, when Apollonius jumped up and said, 'But this coward does not understand either Euripides or me.'

6. News came that Domitian had really distinguished himself in the way he purified the cult of Vesta at Rome; he had put three of the Vestal Virgins to death on a charge of unchastity and of failure to abstain from intercourse.[11] (These virgins

10. On Harmodius and Aristogeiton, see note on V. 34 above. From Phyle (north of Athens on the road to Thebes) Thrasybulus led an expedition which overturned in 403 B.C. the oligarchic rule of The Thirty, set up at the end of the Peloponnesian War.

11. About A.D. 82 Domitian executed the Oculata sisters and a

were obliged to look after Trojan Athena and her fire in abstinence.) 'If only you too,' said Apollonius, 'could be purified, Sun, of the wicked murders of which the earth is now full.' These things he did not say privately as cowards do but proclaimed and prayed for them in the crowd and in the general view.

7. Domitian had killed one of his kinsmen, Sabinus, and was planning to marry Julia, the wife of the murdered man and the niece of the emperor, since she was one of Titus's daughters.[12] Ephesus was sacrificing on behalf of the marriage when Apollonius interrupted the rites and said, 'Night of the Danaids long ago, how unique you were.'[13]

8. Furthermore, this is how he affected events in Rome. Nerva, who held power wisely after Domitian, was thought a suitable candidate for it, and the same belief was held about Orfitus and Rufus.[14] Domitian charged them all with plotting against himself, and had the first two confined to islands, while he ordered Nerva to live in Tarentum.[15] Apollonius had been their friend during the time when Titus ruled with his father and after him, and was always communicating with them

---

certain Varronilla, all Vestal Virgins, for unchastity (cf. Suetonius, *Domitian* 8. 4). Later he also eliminated the chief Vestal, Cornelia.

12. T. Flavius Sabinus, a son of Vespasian's brother, was consul in A.D. 82. He was killed by Domitian because a herald had mistakenly proclaimed him emperor instead of consul.

13. According to legend, the fifty daughters of Danaus had, with one exception, slaughtered their husbands in a single night.

14. Nerva reigned after Domitian from A.D. 96–8. Orfitus must be the Salvidienus Orfitus mentioned by Suetonius (*Domitian* 10. 2) as suspected by Domitian and therefore exiled and murdered. The Rufus is presumably L. Verginius Rufus, an old man (like Nerva himself) who reached a third consulate under Nerva and with the emperor as his colleague.

15. See Introduction, p. 18 above.

about moderation to make them loyal to those emperors, who were virtuous. When Domitian proved harsh, however, Apollonius began to make these men disaffected and to encourage them to achieve the liberation of all. He decided that advice sent by letter would not be safe for them, because many members of the government had been betrayed by their slaves, friends and wives, and no house could keep a secret at that time. So on different occasions he took aside certain of his most discreet followers and said, 'I am making you the bearer of a glorious secret. You must go to so-and-so in Rome, speak with him, and have as much influence to persuade him as I do.' But when he heard that these men had been exiled for showing some kind of hostility to the emperor but lacking the courage to carry through their plans, he gave a discourse about the Fates and Necessity near the grove in Smyrna where the statue of the river Meles is.

9. Knowing that Nerva would be ruler very soon, he had come to the part of his discourse in which he was saying that even tyrants could not fight the decisions of the Fates. A bronze statue of Domitian stood by the Meles, and Apollonius called his audience's attention to it with the words, 'You fool, you are greatly mistaken about the Fates and Necessity. Even if you kill the man who is destined to rule after you, he will come to life again.'

These words came to the ears of Domitian through the slanders of Euphrates. No one could tell who on earth was meant by Apollonius's predictions, but the tyrant, to settle his own fears, decided to put the three men to death. He did not want, however, to appear to do so without justification, and so summoned Apollonius to defend himself for his secret communication with them: either he would condemn Apollonius on his arrival, he thought, and avoid the appearance of executing men without trial, since they would be betrayed along with Apollonius: or if Apollonius by some trick escaped his obvious destiny, he would put them to death with all the more reason as if they had been convicted by their partner in crime.

10. While the emperor was planning this, and a letter was already on its way to the governor of Asia for Apollonius to be arrested and sent to Rome, the man of Tyana foresaw it all, with his usual supernatural power. He told his disciples that he needed to make a secret journey, which put them in mind of the reputation of the ancient Abaris,[16] as if Apollonius had a similar plan. He did not even reveal his intention to Damis, but sailed to Achaea with him. There he disembarked at Corinth, and after his usual midday worship of the sun set sail for Sicily and the land of Italy about evening. Because of the favourable wind he got, and a kind of favouring current that carried him over the sea, he reached Dicaearchia in four days.[17]

. . . . .

16. On the third day after their departure from Dicaearchia they put in at the mouth of the Tiber, from which it is a short sail up to Rome. The person then in charge of the emperor's sword was Aelianus, a man who had long admired Apollonius from the time when he met him in Egypt.[18] He did not speak

16. Abaris was said to have travelled round the world on an arrow: cf. Herodotus IV. 36.

17. Dicaearchia is Puteoli, near Naples.

18. This is Casperius Aelianus, who served as prefect of the praetorian guard some time in the later years of Domitian's reign (about A.D. 93, it would seem). Although he was not prefect at the time Domitian was assassinated (both prefects then were allegedly implicated in the conspiracy), he was again in office under Nerva in A.D. 97: he led a revolt of the praetorian soldiery, which had remained faithful to the memory of Domitian. The reappearance of Aelianus as prefect under Nerva supports the picture of him given by Philostratus, but his role in the uprising of 97 is less consistent with it; possibly the soldiers forced his hand, or Nerva (and Philostratus) misunderstood him.

openly on his behalf before Domitian, since his office did not allow it: he could never have praised to the emperor a man supposed to be his enemy, or interceded for him as a friend of his own. But he used every possible device to help Apollonius secretly. In fact even in the time Apollonius was being attacked before his arrival, Aelianus said, 'Emperor, sophists are talkative creatures, boastful about their skill. Because they get no real pleasure out of living they long for death, and rather than wait for it to come in due course they try to induce it by provoking those that carry swords. That was in Nero's mind, I believe, when he refused to be provoked by Demetrius into taking his life. He knew that he wanted death, and so remitted his death-sentence not out of pardon but because he thought it not worth while to execute him. Musonius the Etruscan, too, often opposed Nero's rule, but the emperor confined him on the island called Gyara. The Greeks are so devoted to these sophists that on that occasion they all sailed to visit him, and now do so to see the fountain. The island had been waterless before, but Musonius discovered a fountain about which the Greeks have as many stories as they do about the horse's fountain on Helicon.'[19]

17. With these words, Aelianus tried to divert the emperor before Apollonius's arrival, but after it he tried a cleverer ruse. He ordered Apollonius to be arrested and brought to him, and when the man who had fabricated the charge attacked Apollonius as a magician of great powers, Aelianus said, 'Save yourself and your charges for the emperor's court.' Apollonius, however, said, 'If I am a magician, how can I be a defendant? And if a defendant, how can I be a magician? But perhaps he thinks the power of informers is so great that even magicians yield to it.'

The accuser wanted to say something even more stupid, but

19. That is, the Hippocrene, often mentioned in ancient literature.

Aelianus stopped him with the words, 'You must allow me the time before the trial, as I want to test the sophist's opinions privately and away from your presence. If he confesses his crime, that will shorten the speeches in court and you will leave in peace. If he makes a reply, the emperor will be the judge.' So Aelianus proceeded to the secret court in which important matters are both brought to light and concealed, and said, 'Everyone will depart, and there must be no witness, since that is the emperor's wish.'

18. When they were alone, Aelianus said, 'Apollonius, I was a boy at the time when the emperor's father came to Egypt to sacrifice to the gods and obtain an oracle from you about his prospects. I was in the retinue of the emperor as a tribune, already having some experience of war, and you were so friendly to me as to take me aside privately when the emperor was occupied with the cities, and tell me my origin, my name and my father's name, and you also predicted to me that I would hold this office. Most people think it is so powerful, more so than all other powers on earth combined, but I find it a burden and a curse. I am appointed to guard an unpopular tyranny, and if I cause its fall I fear the vengeance of heaven. But at least I have shown you my goodwill: for a man who speaks as I have done you can be sure will have undying regard for you, as long as he can remember those kindnesses of yours. My saying that I wished to question you privately about the prosecution's charges was a well-meant device to enable me to talk with you. I want you to feel confidence as far as I am concerned and to be forewarned about the emperor. What his verdict on you will be I do not know, but his attitude is that of a man who wants to condemn but is hesitant to do so on false grounds. He is making you his excuse to execute men of consular rank, because what he wants is forbidden, and so he is achieving it by giving it a veneer of legal appearance. I also

must pretend to be hostile to you: if he suspects that I am trying to acquit you, it is hard to say which of us will die first.'

19. To this Apollonius replied, 'This is an honest conversation we are having. You have told me everything you have in your heart, and I shall do so too. You have a philosophic attitude to your own position, as much as my keenest pupils, and indeed you are so kind to me as to consider yourself implicated in my dangers. So I will tell you my feelings. I could have escaped from all of you into many parts of the world where you have no authority. I could have visited wise men, more wise than myself, and served the gods in righteousness by joining the society of holier people than there are here. Among them there are no indictments, no accusations: for the simple reason that as they neither commit nor suffer injustice they need no courts of justice. Nevertheless, I wanted to avoid being blamed for treachery if I failed to appear in my own defence, while those I had induced to take risks died. I have come to defend myself, therefore, and you must tell me what I must defend myself against.'

20. 'The counts of the indictment,' said Aelianus, 'are various and several. They charge you because of your dress, your habits, with receiving obeisance from some people, and for giving an oracle once in Ephesus about a plague.[20] You are supposed to have spoken against the emperor in secret, in public, or with a claim to divine guidance. One charge is the least plausible of all to me, since I know that you do not tolerate the blood even of sacrificial animals, but to the emperor it is the most plausible. It is said that you went to Nerva's estates, and accompanied a sacrifice he was making against the emperor by slaughtering an Arcadian boy; they

20. cf. IV. 10 above.

say that by means of these rites you built up his hopes, and that all this was done by night when the month was near its end. This charge is much graver than the other ones, and we must remember that it is not unconnected with them. By criticizing your clothes, your habits and your foreknowledge, he is clearly leading up to this other charge and claiming that they gave you the idea of committing crimes against the emperor and the courage to make this sacrifice. You must prepare a defence against all these counts, while your language must not show disrespect for the emperor.'

'I do not have disrespect for him,' said Apollonius, 'as you can see from my coming to defend myself. Even if my powers gave me such confidence that I could look down on tyrannies, I would still have submitted to you, a virtuous man and a friend. There is nothing wrong in being thought a coward by one's enemy, because the hatred of enemies comes not from public accusations but private offences. But to be blamed by a friend for appearing cowardly is something more dreadful than all your enemies' deeds put together. You cannot fail to be detested for your show of cowardice by your friends as well.'

21. Aelianus approved of this speech, and after urging Apollonius to feel confidence, resumed his usual attitude in the knowledge that Apollonius would not be terrified even by the sight of the Gorgon's head. He summoned the men assigned to such duties and said, with a very angry expression, 'My orders are for this man to be kept under guard until the emperor knows of his arrival and of the statements he has made.' He then went to the palace and attended to the duties of his command.

At this point Damis records a story both like and unlike the story of Aristides at Athens. They were expelling Aristides because of his virtue by means of the sherd, and he was already outside the wall when a peasant came up to him and asked him to inscribe a sherd for him against Aristides.[21] The man knew neither Aristides nor the art of writing, but only that he was disliked for being just: Apollonius, on the other hand, was addressed by a tribune who knew him very well, and asked him mockingly the cause of his danger. When Apollonius replied that he did not know, the man said, 'Well, I do. The fact that you received obeisance from human beings has caused you to be accused of receiving the same honours as a god.'

'Who was it who made obeisance to me, then?' asked Apollonius.

'I did,' said the tribune, 'when I was still a boy in Ephesus, when you cured us of the plague.'

'That was very kind of you,' said Apollonius, 'both of you and the cured city.'

'Well, because of that,' said the man, 'I have arranged a defence for you that will free you from the charge. Let us go outside the wall, and if I cut off your head with my sword, the charge will be proved false and you will get an acquittal. But if you terrify me into dropping my sword, we will have to assume that you are supernatural and that the charges are true.' This shows how much less civilized this man was than the one who wanted to exile Aristides; and as he spoke he made faces and laughed. Apollonius appeared not to have

21. This is a reference to the famous story of the early fifth-century Athenian statesman, Aristides, called 'the Just'. He was exiled from Athens in 482 B.C. by the process known as ostracism, named from the sherds (*ostraka*) upon which were incised the names of persons proposed for exile. An illiterate Athenian, not recognizing Aristides, asked him to write the name of Aristides on his sherd; the man said that Aristides had done no wrong, but he was sick of hearing him always called 'the Just'. Aristides obliged. Plutarch tells the story in his life of Aristides, VII. 5–6. Philostratus's remark that Aristides was already outside the wall seems to be a misunderstanding.

heard him, and continued to talk with Damis about the Delta, where they say the Nile divides in two.

22. Aelianus then summoned him, and ordered him to stay in the jail reserved for free men until the emperor had some spare time, since he wanted to have a private meeting with Apollonius before the trial. So Apollonius left the court, and on entering the prison said, 'Let us have a conversation with the people here, Damis. What else is there to do until the time when the tyrant talks with me about his wishes?'

'They will think we are chatterers, if we distract them from preparing their defences, and besides it is tactless to have no regard for people when they are depressed.'

'No,' said Apollonius, 'these people particularly need conversation and comfort. You may remember the lines of Homer in which he makes Helen pour Egyptian potions into the wine to wash away the sorrows of the heart.[22] It seems to me that Helen had a knowledge of Egyptian doctrines with which she charmed the despondent over her mixing-bowl, relieving them with a blend of conversation and wine.'

'Quite likely,' said Damis, 'since she went to Egypt and met Proteus, or in Homer's version became the friend of Polydamna the wife of Thon.[23] However, let us postpone this subject, because I want to ask you something.'

'I know what it is,' said Apollonius; 'you want me to tell you the conversation I had with the prefect and all he said and whether he was fierce or gentle,' and he gave a full account.

Damis fell before him and said, 'Now I believe that Leucothea once gave Odysseus her veil to use after he had lost his ship, when he made his way across the open sea by swimming.[24] We too have fallen into a hopeless and dangerous

22. *Odyssey* IV. 219ff.
23. *Odyssey* IV. 228.
24. *Odyssey* V. 333ff.

situation, but some god is watching over us, I think, to prevent us from losing all hope of rescue.'

Apollonius scolded him for these words. 'How long will you continue with such fears before you realize that wisdom terrifies all those that recognize it, and is terrified by nobody?'

'But the man to whom we have come is ignorant, and so far from being terrified by us that he does not even think there is anything that can terrify him.'

'Well, Damis,' said Apollonius, 'you realize that he is vain and foolish, don't you?'

'Of course I do,' replied Damis.

'Then you must despise the tyrant all the more,' said Apollonius, 'because you understand him.'

. . . . .

27. The next day Apollonius was talking vigorously on the same subject[25] when a man was escorted in, whom Domitian had sent specially to listen to Apollonius's conversations. From his appearance he seemed dejected and claimed to be in great danger; and he was fairly skilled as a speaker, as informers are when they have written eight or ten speeches. Apollonius recognized his profession and conversed on subjects of no use to the man, describing rivers and mountains to his audience and talking of animals and trees, which entertained them but were of no use to the informer. When the man tried to induce Apollonius to attack the emperor, Apollonius said, 'My friend, you can say what you like, since I will not accuse you. I will make my criticisms of the emperor to his face.'

28. There were other episodes in this prison, some of them devised against Apollonius, others fortuitous. They are not important or worth my describing, but Damis recorded them

25. Apollonius had been speaking to his fellow-prisoners on the theme of endurance in adversity.

to ensure completeness, I suppose. The following, however, are relevant. It was the evening of Apollonius's fifth day under guard, when a man who spoke Greek entered the prison.

'Where is the man from Tyana?' he asked. Taking Apollonius aside, he said, 'The emperor will talk with you tomorrow. You may consider this a message from Aelianus.'

'I understand the secret,' said Apollonius, 'since he is the only one that knows it.'

'Moreover,' he said, 'the superintendent of the prison has been instructed to do you any favours you want.'

'You are all very kind,' replied Apollonius, 'but my way of life in here and outside is the same. I talk on any subject that offers, and need nothing.'

'Not even someone to advise you,' the man asked, 'on addressing the emperor, Apollonius?'

'Yes, I do need that,' replied Apollonius, 'as long as he doesn't advise me to use flattery.'

'Suppose he urges you not to despise or disrespect the emperor?' asked the man.

'That would be excellent advice,' answered Apollonius, 'exactly what I had decided on.'

'That is what I have come about,' said the man, 'and I am glad to see you fairly well prepared. But you also have to be ready for the emperor's voice and his surly expression, because his voice is harsh even when he is talking kindly, and his cheek is flushed with anger: this feature is very conspicuous. We must not be afraid of these things, man of Tyana, since they are really natural to him, and do not change.'

'And yet,' replied Apollonius, 'Odysseus went into the Cyclops' cave without any information about the giant's size or diet or booming voice, and still he faced up to him, after his initial fear, and proved himself a man before he left the cave. For me it is enough to leave with my own life and that of the friends because of whom I am in jeopardy.'

After this conversation with the visitor, which he then reported to Damis, Apollonius went to sleep.

29. At daybreak a clerk from the imperial court came and said, 'Apollonius, the emperor asks you to come to court at mid-morning, but not to make your defence; he wants to see exactly what kind of person you are and to talk with you privately.'

'Well,' said Apollonius, 'why are you talking with me about this?'

'You are Apollonius, aren't you?' asked the clerk.

'Yes,' he replied, 'Apollonius of Tyana.'

'Then whom should I give this message to?'

'To those who are going to take me,' said Apollonius, 'because it is a prison that I have to come from.'

'They have already received these orders,' said the clerk, 'and I will return here too when the time comes. For the present I have only come to relay the message, since the orders were issued late last night.'

30. The clerk then left, while Apollonius lay down on his bed and said, 'I need sleep, Damis. I have had a bad night trying to recall something I once heard from Phraotes.'

'But you ought to stay awake, rather,' said Damis, 'and prepare yourself for the appointment, since it is so important.'

'How could I prepare myself,' asked Apollonius, 'when I don't yet know what he is going to ask?'

'Are you going to improvise, then,' asked Damis, 'when your life is at stake?'

'Yes, Damis,' he replied, 'just as I improvise in life itself. But I want to tell you the remark of Phraotes which I recalled, because you will consider it useful in the circumstances too. Phraotes advises that we should not hit the lions which people make pets of, because they bear resentment if they are hit, and we should not spoil them because that makes them capricious. Instead, we should mix caresses with threats, and so educate them to ways of obedience. He was not of course referring to lions, since our conversations were not about raising pets, but giving me a rein to use with tyrants, which he thought would prevent me from leaving the proper path.'

'That saying,' replied Damis, 'is a very appropriate description of a tyrant's character, but there is also in Aesop the lion in the cave, which Aesop says was only pretending to be ill, and caught the animals that came to visit it. But the vixen said, "What am I to make of this creature? Nobody comes away from him: there is no trace of anybody coming out."'

Apollonius replied, 'For myself, I would have thought the vixen more clever if she had gone inside without being caught, and had left the cave making her own traces.'

31. After saying this, he snatched a very short sleep, just as much as settled on his eyes. When day came, he prayed to the Sun, as best he could in a prison, and talked with those who came to him about every subject they asked. Eventually, at mid-morning, the clerk came and said that Apollonius should be at the doors immediately, in case they were called in promptly. 'Let us go,' replied Apollonius, and started out eagerly. As he went, four bodyguards followed him, keeping a greater distance than if they were accompanying him for his safety, and Damis came along also, concealing his fear in a meditative expression.

All the passers-by looked at Apollonius; his clothing in itself drew stares and there was a venerability in his appearance that seemed god-given; besides, the fact that he had come to risk his life for honourable men now won over to him even those who had hated him before. When he arrived at the palace, he saw different men receiving and paying respect and the hubbub of people going in and out, and said, 'This place, Damis, seems to me like a bath-house: I see those outside hurrying to get in and those inside hurrying out, and some look clean and others unclean.' I warn trespassers to keep off this remark and not to ascribe it to this man or that; to such an extent does it belong to Apollonius that it is used by him in a letter.

He saw a very old man eager to be a governor and for that same reason showing servility and waiting on the emperor, and said, 'This man, Damis, has not yet been persuaded by Sophocles to shun his raging, savage master.'[26]

'Yes, Apollonius,' said Damis, 'the very master that we have chosen too: that is why we are standing at such doors as these.'

'You seem to me, Damis,' replied Apollonius, 'to think that these gates are guarded by the same Aeacus as is said to be in Hades, because you look like a dead man.'

'Not a dead man,' replied Damis, 'but a man on the point of death.'

'I have the impression, Damis, that you are unreconciled to death, even though you have been with me a long time, studying philosophy from your youth, and I thought you were ready for it and knew all the discipline I can command. Fighters and heavy-armed soldiers need not only courage but also discipline to divine the turning-points of a battle, and similarly philosophers must watch for the turning-points at which they are to die, so that they may not make for them with indiscipline or recklessness, but with the best judgement. That I have chosen, if someone wishes to kill me, to die at the correct point for a philosopher is a position I have maintained in your presence, but which I am tired of teaching you yourself.'

26. cf. the quotation from Sophocles on the tyranny of sex in Plato's *Republic* 329 C. This remark of the dramatist is also cited above, I. 13.

32. So much for this conversation. Eventually the emperor put aside all immediate business and found time to talk with Apollonius, who was led into the palace by those assigned to such duties. Damis was not allowed to follow him. The emperor was wearing a crown of leaves, having just sacrificed to Athena in the court of Adonis; this was a court full of the pots of flowers which the Assyrians tend inside their houses for use in the rites of Adonis. The emperor turned around from the rites in which he had been engaged and, taken aback by Apollonius's appearance, said, 'Aelianus, you have brought a spirit before me.'

Apollonius was not disturbed, and catching up what he had just heard said, 'I thought Athena had made the same provision for you, emperor, that she once did for Diomedes in Troy. She took away from Diomedes's eyes the mist that prevents men from seeing fully, and gave him the power to distinguish gods and men.[27] But the goddess has not yet purified you in that way, emperor; she should have done, so that you could better see Athena herself and not mistake men for appearances of spirits.'

'And you, philosopher,' said Domitian, 'when did you receive this purification?'

'Long ago,' said Apollonius, 'when I first became a philosopher.'

'Then how is it,' asked Domitian, 'that you consider the men who are my greatest enemies to be gods?'

'What enmity,' asked Apollonius, 'do you have with Iarchas or Phraotes, the Indians? They are the only humans whom I consider gods and worthy of being called so.'

'Don't wander off to the Indians,' said the emperor; 'tell me about your dear friend Nerva and his partners in crime.'

27. cf. *Iliad* V. 127. Domitian had a special regard for the goddess Minerva (i.e. Athena, in Greek): cf. Suetonius, *Domitian* 4. 4 and 15. 3.

'Do you expect me to defend him,' asked Apollonius, ' or –'

'Don't do that,' replied Domitian; 'he has been proved guilty. Prove to me that you are not guilty yourself or aware of any such doings of his.'

'If you want to know what I am aware of, emperor,' replied Apollonius, 'let me tell you. There is no point in concealing the truth.'

The emperor thought he was going to hear a wonderful secret and that everything favoured the dispatch of Apollonius's friends. When Apollonius saw him elated by this supposition, he said, [33] 'I know that Nerva is the most controlled and moderate of men, most loyal to you and a good governor, but so distrustful of power and pomp that he avoids office. His friends, by whom you mean Rufus and Orfitus, I suppose,[28] are also controlled to the best of my knowledge, and ill-disposed to wealth, and too unambitious to do all that they might. They could not plot revolution themselves or join with someone else doing so.'

The emperor was beside himself at these words, and said, 'So you convict me of laying false information against them, do you, calling the same people virtuous and unambitious whom I have found to be utterly depraved and eager for my power? Yes, I suppose if I were to ask them about you they would not admit you were a magician, a bandit, a braggart, a money-grubber, a man who thinks himself above the laws. That's your evil conspiracy, you pack of scoundrels. But the trial will bring everything out. I know all you swore to do, and why you made that sacrifice and when and what it was, just as if I had been there to join in.'

Apollonius was not cowed by this either, and said, 'It is a disgrace and a violation of the laws to judge a case in which you are convinced, or to be convinced of a case in which you

28. cf. VII. 8, above.

are yet to judge. If this is so, let me begin my defence this way. You are mistaken in your opinion about me, emperor, and you do me more wrong than the man who perjures himself accusing me, because before you have heard it you believe what he said he would prove to you.'

'Begin your defence where you like,' said Domitian, 'but I know immediately both where it will end and how it ought to begin.'

34. At this point he began his outrages against Apollonius, having his beard cut off and his hair, and putting him in the prison for the lowest criminals. Apollonius said about being shaved, 'I had not realized, emperor, that I was on trial because of my hair,' and about being enchained, 'If you think I am a magician, how will you keep me in chains? And if you keep me in chains, how will you be able to say I am a magician?'

'I will not free you,' replied Domitian, 'before you turn into water, or some animal or tree.'

'I would not turn into such things,' replied Apollonius, 'even if I could; I would never betray those completely innocent men brought to trial. I will be myself, and subject myself to everything you may do to this body of mine until I have defended my friends.'

'Whom do you expect to defend you?' asked the emperor.

'Time,' said Apollonius, 'the inspiration of god, and the love of my companion, wisdom.'

35. This is how Damis describes the first round of Apollonius's defence, the part that involved him and Domitian alone. Writers who have given a malicious version of these events say that Apollonius defended himself first and was only imprisoned later, and that it was then too that he was shaved. They have invented a letter written in the Ionic dialect and of

tedious prolixity in which they pretend that Apollonius implored Domitian and asked to be freed from his bonds. Apollonius wrote his will in Ionic, but a letter of his in that dialect I have never come across, though I have made a large collection of them, and I never observed verbosity in one of his letters; they are all as brief as if they were deciphered from code. Moreover, he left the court after winning his case, and how could he have been imprisoned after a vote for acquittal? I do not, however, want to mention the court yet: I must mention first what followed after his being shaved and his various discourses, because they are worth reporting.

36. He had been in prison for two days when a man came there who claimed to have bribed his way in to see him, and to have come to advise him for his own safety. This man was from Syracuse, and was the mind and the tongue of Domitian. He was an agent like the previous one, but more plausible because the other man tried to catch Apollonius before his troubles, but this one had the circumstances to help him.

'Heavens,' he said, 'who would have expected Apollonius to be in chains?'

'The man who put me there,' was the reply, 'because he would not have put me in chains if he hadn't.'

'Who would have expected his lovely hair would ever be cut off?' the Syracusan said.

'I who grew it,' said Apollonius.

'How are you taking all this?'

'As you would expect me to,' said Apollonius, 'since I came to face it neither willingly nor unwillingly.'

'How is your leg taking the pain?' the man asked.

'I don't know,' replied Apollonius; 'my mind is on something else.'

'But your mind must be on your pain,' said the other.

'Not at all,' replied Apollonius; 'the mind of a man with my character will either feel no pain or stop the pain.'

'What is your mind occupied with, then?'

'Precisely with avoiding all thought of the present.'

The man kept referring to his hair again, and brought the conversation round to it, until Apollonius said, 'It is a good thing for you, young man, that you were not one of the Greeks at Troy. I think you would have grieved terribly for the hair of Achilles when he cut it for Patroclus, if that is what he did, in fact you would have swooned over it. If you say you are sorry for my hair, which was turning grey and dull, what would you have felt about his hair, which was blond and carefully groomed?'

The man had really spoken with malicious intent to find out what caused Apollonius pain, and better still to see if he would speak ill of the emperor for what he had done to him. But he was brought short by what Apollonius said, and continued, 'There are many things of which you have been accused before the emperor, above all because of the crimes for which Nerva and others are being charged; but he has also heard accusations about speeches which you made in Ionia opposing and attacking him. He does not care about these, I am told, because his anger is concentrated on the graver charges, even though the person who made the other ones is a man of considerable reputation.'

'You would think he was an Olympic victor, the way he thinks he has got a "reputation" through the power of slander. I know it is Euphrates. I am aware he is doing everything to harm me, and I have already suffered a greater injustice from him. He once heard that I was planning to visit the Naked Philosophers in Egypt and resorted to slandering me to them.[29] If I had not understood his design, I might perhaps have left without even seeing those gentlemen.'

29. On Euphrates's plot to slander Apollonius to the Naked Philosophers, see above, VI. 7ff.

The man from Syracuse was amazed at his words, and said, 'So you think it is less important to be accused before the emperor than for the Naked Philosophers not to think you virtuous because of Euphrates's gossip?'

'Of course,' replied Apollonius. 'I went there to learn, but I have come here to instruct.'

'What is the subject of your instruction?' the man asked.

'The fact that I am an honourable man, which is something that the emperor does not yet know.'

'You are in a position,' replied the other, 'to help yourself by telling him certain things that would have saved you from being imprisoned, if you had said them before you came here.'

Apollonius realized that the man was urging him to say something similar to what the emperor had said, and that he thought that the desire to escape his bonds would make him tell lies against the others. So he said, 'My friend, if telling Domitian the truth has put me in prison, what will happen to me if I do not tell it? He thinks the truth deserves imprisonment, but I think lying does.'

37. The man from Syracuse admired him as a 'thorough philosopher', those being the words he used before parting, and so he left the prison. Apollonius looked at Damis and said, 'Do you understand this Python?'

'I understand,' Damis replied, 'that he was trying to trap and entice you, but what you mean by "Python" and what the significance of the word is, escapes me.'

'There once was a Python of Byzantium,' said Apollonius, 'a good speaker for a wicked subject. He came as an ambassador of Philip the son of Amyntas to the Greeks in the hope of making them slaves. He did not bother about most of them, but in Athens itself, when the art of rhetoric was at its height there, he said that they were doing wrong to Philip and that the Athenians were committing an outrage in making the

Greeks free. That is what Python said "in a flood of eloquence", so it is reported, but Demosthenes of Paeania was the only one to answer his arrogance, and counts the fact that he checked him among his own achievements.[30] I would never call it my achievement not to be enticed to do what this man wanted, but I meant that he was acting like Python because he came in the pay of a tyrant and with unacceptable advice.'

38. Damis says that Apollonius gave other discourses of the sort, while he himself was baffled by their predicament and saw no way out of it, except the kind that the gods have granted to some people's prayers in much worse circumstances. Shortly before noon he said to him, 'Man of Tyana,' (since Apollonius liked very much to be addressed this way) 'what will happen to us?'

'What has already happened,' replied Apollonius, 'and nothing more. No one will kill us.'

'Who is so invulnerable as that?' asked Damis. 'And when will you be freed?'

'As far as my judge is concerned, today,' was the reply, 'but as far as I am, immediately.'

So saying, he took his leg out of its shackle and said to Damis, 'I have given you proof of my freedom. Be courageous.'

At that moment, says Damis, he first understood clearly that Apollonius's nature was godlike and more than human. Without sacrificing, which of course he could not do in prison, or praying, or saying anything, he belittled his chains and then put his leg back in them and acted like a prisoner.

30. Python of Byzantium went to Athens as ambassador of Philip II of Macedon in 343 B.C. For Demosthenes's comment on his own role, cf. *On the Crown*, 136.

39. Less intelligent people ascribe such acts to magic, and in fact have the same idea about many spheres of human action. Athletes call on this art, and so do all competitors because of their greed for victory. It does not give them any help towards winning, but when chance gives them victories these poor fools deprive themselves of the credit and assign it to this art of magic. Even those who lose to them do not lose faith in it, because they say and think, 'If I had made this sacrifice and burned that incense, victory would not have eluded me.'

This art also visits the houses of merchants. They too can be found ascribing their successes in trade to the magician, but reverses to their own meanness and failure to make all the proper sacrifices. It is lovers above all that this art battens on to. The disease they have is such an impressionable one that they talk to old hags about it, and so it is no surprise, I think, that they go to these quacks and take such advice from them. These men tell them to wear amulets and stones which come from the recesses of the earth, from the moon or the stars, and every spice that India produces; and while they exact a fine fee from them for all this, they do not help them at all. Suppose a catamite shows some affection for his lover, or is swayed by presents, and the affair makes progress: the lover praises magic as if it can do anything. Suppose the attempt fails: he blames some omission, there was this or that which he did not burn or sacrifice or melt, and this is some crucial but unobtainable ingredient. The ways in which they manufacture signs from heaven and many other such things have actually been described by some people who hold magic in utter contempt. It is enough for me to advise the young not to be influenced even by this second class of men, so that they do not learn to consider such things so much as a joke. That is a long enough digression from my account. Why should I spend more time attacking a practice which is abhorrent both to nature and to law?

40. Apollonius had revealed himself to Damis and spoken further, when a man came up about noon and delivered the following message by word of mouth: 'The emperor is releasing you from these bonds immediately, Apollonius, on the advice of Aelianus, and permits you to stay in the free men's prison until you make your defence. That will be in four days' time, perhaps.'

'Who will conduct me from here?' asked Apollonius.

'I will,' said the man; 'follow me.'

When those in the free men's prison saw him, they all embraced him, since he had come back quite contrary to their expectations. Children love their father for correcting them kindly and moderately, or telling stories of his youth, and in the same way these loved Apollonius and confessed as much to him, and he was constantly giving them advice.

41. The next day he called Damis and said, 'My defence will occur on the appointed day, but you must take the road to Dicaearchia,[31] because it is better to go by land, and if you talk to Demetrius, walk by the sea where the isle of Calypso is, because I will appear before your eyes there.'

'Alive,' asked Damis, 'or how?'

Apollonius laughed and said, 'To my way of thinking, alive, but to yours, risen from the dead.'

Damis says he left unwillingly, neither dreading that Apollonius would die nor confident that he would not. In two days he reached Dicaearchia, and heard about the storm that had occurred at that time. A rainstorm had broken over the sea, and sunk some ships that were sailing to the city and driven others to Sicily and the Straits. Then Damis understood why Apollonius had told him to travel by land.

31. i.e. Puteoli.

42. What follows Damis describes from the account which he had from Apollonius in conversation with Demetrius and himself. A conspicuously good-looking boy from Messene in Arcadia came to Rome, and caused many to fall in love with him: above all, Domitian, but the others were so much in love that they did not even fear having Domitian as a rival. The boy, however, was chaste and kept his good looks to himself. That he despised gold, money, horses, or other such enticements as some people use to seduce boys, is no reason for us to praise him, because a true man should be prepared for such things; but this boy would have been more highly rewarded than all the boys together whom the eyes of rulers ever caused to be dragged off, and even so he did not put the price on himself that others did. So he was put into prison by the decision of his lover. He came up to Apollonius, looking as if he wanted to say something, but his modesty advised him to keep silent, and he did not have the courage. Apollonius understood, and said, 'You are not yet of an age to be a criminal, and yet you are in prison, just like us poor people.'

'Yes,' said the boy, 'and I am going to die, because nowadays the laws make death the wages of chastity.'

'So did the laws in the time of Theseus,' said Apollonius; 'he put his own son to death in a matter of chastity.'[32]

'My father,' replied the boy, 'has caused my death too. Although I was an Arcadian of Messene, he did not give me a Greek education, but sent me here to learn legal science. It was for this that I had come when the emperor saw me, to my detriment.'

Apollonius, as if he did not understand, said, 'Tell me,

32. The reference is to the father of Hippolytus; Phaedra fell in love with the youth, who was her stepson. Theseus cursed Hippolytus, under the false impression that he was unchaste, and invoked Poseidon, who sent a bull from the sea to kill him.

young man, does the emperor think you are grey-eyed, though I see you have dark eyes, or does he think you have a hooked nose, though you are perfectly formed, like a naked herm, or that your hair is other than it is? I think it is radiant and shining, and your lips are so shaped as to be formed both for silence and for speech, and your neck is so free and proud. Which of these does the emperor think to be other than as it is, since you say that he saw you to your detriment?'

'It is precisely this which has ruined me. He has fallen in love with me, but will not leave the things he praises alone. He intends to dishonour me as men in love with women do.'

Apollonius admired him, and passed over such questions as his opinion of intercourse and whether it was immoral or not, because he saw the Arcadian blushing and using modest language. So he asked him, 'Do you have some slaves in Arcadia?'

'Why, many,' was the reply.

'What do you think your relation is to them?' asked Apollonius.

'What the laws think,' he replied; 'I am their master.'

'Should slaves be obedient to their masters,' asked Apollonius, 'or refuse the wishes of those that possess their bodies?'

The boy realized the answer that he was being led to, and said, 'I know that the power of tyrants is irresistible and strong, because that is why they claim to be the masters of the free. But I am the master of my own body, and I will keep it uncorrupted.'

'How?' asked Apollonius; 'You are dealing with a lover who pursues your beauty with a sword.'

'I will choose to bend my neck to him, since that is what he wants with a sword.'

Apollonius approved, and said, 'I see you are an Arcadian.' Moreover, he mentions this boy in a letter, and describes him much more beautifully than I do here. He praises him for his continence to the person he is writing to, and says that he was not killed by the tyrant, but won admiration for his firmness, and so sailed back to Malea. He was more of a hero in Arcadia than those who win the endurance test of the whips at Sparta.[33]

33. The training of young Spartan males included floggings, which were sometimes fatal.

BOOK VIII

1. Let us go into the court to hear Apollonius defending himself against the charge. The sun is rising, and the chief citizens are now permitted to enter the court. The emperor's intimates say that he has not tasted food, because (I suppose) he is reading over the contents of the case; in fact, he holds a document in his hand and is at one moment angry, at another less so. We must imagine him as it were resentful against the laws because they provided for courts.

2. We will also meet Apollonius planning to have a discussion rather than run a race with his life at stake, as we can tell from what happened outside the court-house. As Apollonius walked, he asked the clerk who was leading him where they were going, and when the clerk said he was leading him to the court-house, Apollonius said, 'Whom am I appearing in court against?'

'Against your accuser, and the case will be judged by the emperor.'

'But who will judge between me and the emperor? I am going to convict him of doing wrong to philosophy.'

'What concern does an emperor have with philosophy, even if he proves to do wrong to it?'

'But philosophy has a great concern with an emperor, to make him rule well.'

The clerk approved of this; in fact he had been fairly well-disposed towards Apollonius, as he showed from the start.

'How much water will you want to measure your speech?'

he asked.[1] 'This is something I have to know before the trial.'

'If I am allowed to say as much as the trial demands, the Tiber itself would be measured out sooner: but if I am only allowed to speak in reply to the emperor's questions, the limit of my reply will be set by my questioner.'

'You must have studied two opposing skills if you claim that you can speak briefly and lengthily on the same subject.'

'They are not opposing skills,' said Apollonius, 'but similar. A man who mastered one of them would also be proficient in the other. And a balanced combination of the two would be, not a third skill in speaking, but the first. I know too that a fourth skill is that of being silent in court.'

'A profitless one,' said the clerk, 'for you and anybody about to stand trial.'

'Still,' said Apollonius, 'it brought great profit to Socrates of Athens, when he was the defendant in his case.'

'How did it profit him,' asked the other, 'since his silence led to his death?'

'He did not die,' replied Apollonius, 'even if the Athenians thought so.'

3. In this way he was prepared for anything the tyrant did. As he stood before the court-house, another clerk came up and said, 'Man of Tyana, take everything off and then go in.'

'Are we having a bath or a trial?' asked Apollonius.

'This warning does not refer to clothes,' said the other; 'the emperor forbids you to bring in here any amulet, paper, or any other document.'

'Not even a cane for the person who gave him this idiotic advice?' asked Apollonius.

His accuser shouted out, 'Emperor, the magician is threatening to beat me, because it was I that gave you this advice.'

1. A water-clock was used for timing speeches in court.

'In that case,' said Apollonius, 'it is you that is the magician, not I, because you claim to have advised the emperor that I am something which I have yet to advise him that I am not.'

Beside the accuser, as he hurled this abuse, was a freedman of Euphrates. Euphrates is said to have sent him to report Apollonius's discourses in Ionia, and also to have supplied him with money which was handed over to the accuser.

4. These were their skirmishes before the trial, and the course of it was as follows. The court-house had been arranged as if to accommodate an audience for a rhetorical display. All the famous people were there, since the emperor was at pains to have as large an audience as possible when Apollonius was convicted in order to convict the others. Apollonius was so contemptuous of the emperor that he did not even look at him. His accuser attacked his contempt, and told him to keep his eyes 'on the god of all mankind', whereupon Apollonius turned his eyes to the ceiling, to show that he had his eyes on Zeus and had a lower opinion of the object of this impious flattery than of the flatterer. The accuser also shouted, 'Start measuring out the water now, emperor. If you allow him a long speech, he will choke us. I also have a paper with the charges written on it to which he must speak. Make him give his defence to one of these at a time.'

The emperor thanked the man for this excellent advice and ordered Apollonius to make his defence as the informer advised. He passed over most of the charges as not worth making anybody answer, but questioned him as follows about four, which he thought conclusive and impossible to answer.

'What knowledge do you have, Apollonius,' he asked, 'that makes you wear different clothing from everyone else, peculiar and conspicuous?'

'It is because the earth that feeds me also clothes me,' replied Apollonius, 'and I do not bother poor animals.'

Next, the emperor asked, 'Why is it that men call you a god?'

'Because every man who is considered good is honoured with the title of "god".' Where Apollonius got this philosophic idea I have shown in my account of the Indians.[2]

Third, he asked him about the disease at Ephesus. 'On what basis, with what evidence, did you predict to the Ephesians that they would have the plague?'

'I have a lighter diet, emperor, and so was the first to sense the danger. But if you like, I will tell you what causes plagues.' Domitian, I suppose, was afraid that Apollonius would ascribe such diseases to his own injustice, his incestuous relationship[3] and his other unnatural acts, and so he said, 'I do not want that kind of answer.' When he began to aim his fourth question at Apollonius's friends, he did not start in immediately, but waited for a long time deep in thought; then, as if he were dizzy, he asked a question quite unlike what they all expected. The audience thought he would drop his pretence and not avoid naming the others, and would vent his fury about the sacrifice. Instead he crept up on the question by saying, 'Tell me, when you had left the house on such and such a day, and gone to the country, for whom did you sacrifice the boy?'

Apollonius, as if he were scolding a child, said, 'Shame on you! If I left the house, I visited the country; and if this, I sacrificed; and if this, I ate. But let those who deserve credit testify to it.' When Apollonius said this, greater applause

2. Above, III. 18 (with a cross-reference by Philostratus to this passage).

3. Domitian lived openly with his niece Julia, Titus's daughter. His lawful wife was Domitia Longina, daughter of the great Neronian general, Corbulo. Philostratus's word here is *gamous*, which would normally (though not necessarily) mean 'marriage'; hence, Philostratus *may* have been under a misapprehension about Julia and Domitian. cf. above, VII. 7.

broke out than the emperor's court allows, and the emperor, thinking that the audience was giving testimony on Apollonius's behalf, and somewhat affected by the firmness and the good sense of his replies, said, 'I acquit you of the charges, but you must remain until we have conversed privately.'

Apollonius, however, gathered his courage and said, 'Thank you, emperor, but because of these god-forsaken men the cities are ruined, the islands are full of fugitives, the mainland of groaning, the armies of cowardice, and the senate of suspicion. Allow me, too, leave to speak, if that be your wish; if not, send someone to take hold of my body, because to take hold of my soul is impossible. In fact, you can never even take hold of my body; "you will not kill me, since I am not mortal".'[4]

With these words he vanished from the court-house, and took advantage of the present opportunity because the tyrant was evidently planning to question him on a variety of subjects rather than in good faith, no doubt being proud of the fact that he had not put him to death; and Apollonius was anxious not to be led into such an examination. He thought that the best way to ensure this was not to conceal his nature but to make clear that he was able never to be caught if he did not want it. Moreover, his fears for the others had now been allayed, because the tyrant had never even ventured to question him about them, and he could not plausibly put them to death on a charge that had not stood up in court. This is what I have found about the course of the trial.

. . . . .

6. Apollonius also composed a speech to recite in his defence during his allotted time; but since the tyrant confined him to the questions I have mentioned, I must write out his speech at this point. I am aware that it will be criticized by admirers of

4. *Iliad* XXII. 13.

vulgar styles, because it has less polish than they say is necessary, and is overdone in its vocabulary and ideas. But when I consider Apollonius, I do not think a wise man would correctly represent his own character by cultivating clauses of equal length or antitheses, and making his tongue clack like a rattle. These things are the hallmark of professional rhetoricians, and even they do not need them. Obvious cleverness in court can harm a man's cause by making him appear to be laying a trap for the jurors; while the concealed kind may leave the court-house with a favourable verdict: to hide from the judges how clever you are is the truer kind of cleverness. When a wise man defends himself, however (a wise man will not accuse, since he has the power to amend), he needs a manner different from those of lawyers, a style that is practised without appearing so, and he himself must be rather grave and little short of contemptuous; his speech should avoid raising pity, since a man who cannot bring himself to make entreaties could never speak with the purpose of raising pity. That is how this speech will seem to all who listen to me and Apollonius with their taste uncorrupted. This is how it went.

7. (1) 'You and I, emperor, are playing for high stakes. You are running a risk that no emperor ever did before, if you prove to be an enemy of philosophy with no just cause. I am running one that even Socrates of Athens did not run. Those who indicted him held that he had strange beliefs about spiritual matters, but did not call him a spirit himself, or believe he was one.

'Since both of us are exposed to so great a risk, I will not hesitate to give you advice of which I am convinced. Since the accuser brought us to this trial, most people have formed an incorrect opinion about me and you. They decided that you were going to let your anger decide your judgement, and because of it would be prepared to execute me, whatever

execution is. They decided that I was going to put myself out
of reach of justice by all the means that exist for running
away, which are numerous. When I heard this, I was not led
to be prejudiced against you, or to condemn your judgement
as less than upright; I obeyed the laws, and I am standing trial.
The advice I want to give you is the same. It is fair not to be
prejudiced, nor to sit in judgement already convinced that I
have done you some wrong. The Armenians, the Babylonians,
and all those that rule in that region have many horsemen,
huge numbers of archers, gold-bearing lands, and a host of
brave men, as I well know: and yet it would make you laugh
to hear that they were going to do you some harm which
would actually deprive you of this empire of yours. It is not
fair, therefore, to be convinced that one wise man unarmed
has a weapon against the emperor of Rome, and to accept such
a story from the lips of an Egyptian informer. You have never
heard such a thing from Athena, the goddess who you say is
your protector. But perhaps after all the arts of flattery and
informing have now been brought to such a stage of cultiva-
tion by these brigands that you consider the gods able to give
you advice on minor matters such as inflammation of the eyes
and how to avoid fever and to stop your intestines swelling,
so that they treat you and attend to you like doctors; whereas
on the subject of dangers to your power or your person, you
do not think them able to advise you whom to be on your
guard against or to come and tell you what will protect you
from such people. Informers are now the shield of Athena and
the hand of Zeus to you. They claim to know things about
your protection which the gods are ignorant of, and their
waking and sleeping lives are dedicated to you, if in fact they
get any sleep, always joining "disaster to disaster", as the
saying is, and constantly plotting their interminable crimes.
They may own stables, wheel into the forum drawn by white
horses, and dine off silver and gold; they may buy catamites

for twenty or thirty thousand drachmas; they may be adulterers as long as they are not caught and marry the women they have corrupted when they are taken in the act; they may win applause for their distinguished triumphs when an innocent philosopher or consular is ruined by them and executed by you, but let us ascribe this to the damnable creatures' extravagance and their loss of all respect for the laws or for the public eye. But the fact that they claim to have more prescience than the gods is something that I cannot praise, and indeed tremble to hear it; and if you are to believe it they may perhaps indict you for impugning religious beliefs, since you may well become the object of such indictments when there is no one else left for informers to inform against. I know well that I am making criticisms rather than a defence, but I wanted to say this about the laws, which you must consider your governors if you are to govern.

(2) 'Who will support me in my defence? If I were to invoke Zeus as whose servant I know I have lived, they will say I am a magician and am bringing the sky down to the earth. So let us discuss this matter with a man who is generally thought to be dead, though not by me: your father.[5] I was as valuable to him as he was to you, because he made you what you are, and I made him what he was. He, emperor, will be my supporter in my defence, and indeed he knows me better than you do. He came to Egypt before he was emperor to sacrifice to the gods of the country and to discuss his position with me.[6] Although he found me with my long hair and dressed as I am, he never asked me a single question about my appearance, because he thought highly of everything about me. It was to see me that he admitted having come, and when he left he thanked me; he had said things to me which he said to nobody else and had been told things which nobody

5. Vespasian, who died in A.D. 79.
6. cf. V. 27ff., above.

else had told him. His resolve to take power was strengthened by me more than anyone else, though it was already wavering under the effect of other men who had his interests at heart – though you might not think so, since those who urged him not to take power were in effect robbing you of the chance to have the same power after him. However, I advised him not to think himself unworthy of power, when it had come begging to him, and to take the two of you as his heirs;[7] and it was because he admitted the value of this advice that he grew to greatness himself and raised you both to it too. But if he had thought me a magician he would not have discussed his worries with me. He did not come and say such things as "Compel the Fates or Zeus to make me tyrant" or "Produce a miracle for me by showing the sun rising in the west and setting where it rises." I would not have thought him fit to rule either for ascribing such powers to me or for using tricks to ensnare power, when he ought to use his virtues to win it.

'Besides, I talked to him publicly in a sanctuary, whereas magicians avoid the sanctuaries of gods for their appointments, since these are unpropitious for the practice of their art. They screen themselves in night or any place that lacks illumination to prevent their stupid clients from having either eyes or ears.

'I also talked with him privately, though with Euphrates and Dio present. Of these the first is extremely hostile to me, and the other extremely friendly, and I hope I may never cease counting Dio among my friends. Well, who would talk of magic before wise men, or at any rate pretenders to wisdom? Would not anybody avoid revealing his wickedness, whether before enemies or friends? Our conversation, too, was completely unlike those about magic. You may think that your own father so desired the throne that he trusted magicians rather than himself, and obtained from me a means to compel the gods so that he could obtain it. In fact he already

7. i.e., Titus and Domitian, Vespasian's sons.

considered himself to be in possession of it before he reached
Egypt, and thereafter talked with me on more important
subjects: laws, and the just use of wealth, and he was eager
to learn how he should worship the gods and what blessings
they gave to rulers who observed the laws. These are things to
which magicians as a species are entirely opposed, because the
prevalence of such practices would destroy the art of magic.

(3) 'There is something else, too, emperor, which you
should keep in mind. All the arts that exist on earth have
different spheres, but all have the object of money, whether
little or much or simply enough to subsist on. This includes not
only menial arts but all the others too, the wise ones and the
fairly wise ones alike, except for that of true wisdom. By
"wise" arts I mean those of poetry, music, astronomy, teaching and rhetoric except of the forensic kind, and by "fairly
wise" those of painting, sculpture, of statue-makers, pilots,
farmers as long as they obey the seasons, since these arts too are
not far removed from wisdom. But there is also, emperor,
something in false philosophers and in pedlars which one
should not suppose to be prophecy, because that is very valuable if it proves correct, though whether it is an art I do not
know. In any case I consider magicians to be false philosophers,
because the belief that what does not exist does, and the
refusal to believe in what does exist, all this I ascribe to the
states of mind of the poor creatures they deceive. Whatever is
wise in magic depends on the stupidity of those that are tricked
and make sacrifices. The practitioners of the art are all avari-
cious; all their clever devices they have invented for the sake of
profit; and they chase after enormous sums of money by
deceiving people who have any kind of craving and by pretending that they have unlimited powers. Is it because you see
me in possession of wealth that you think I practise false
philosophy despite your own father, who thought me above
money? To prove that I am telling the truth, let me find the

letter from that excellent and inspired man. In it he extols me for my poverty, as well as for other qualities.

"The emperor Vespasian greets the philosopher Apollonius.

"If everyone were willing to be a philosopher of your kind, Apollonius, that would be a great good fortune both for philosophy and for poverty. Philosophy would be incorruptible and poverty independent. Good-bye."

'Let that be the defence of me made by your father, who ascribed to me incorruptibility in my philosophy and independence in my poverty. No doubt he remembered what had happened in Egypt, when Euphrates and many who claimed to be philosophers approached him openly with requests for money, whereas I, so far from approaching him for money, tried to deter the others too for their improper conduct: I was an enemy of money even as a young man. I had seen my inheritance, which consisted of a wealthy estate, for only one day when I gave it to my brothers and friends and the poor among my relatives, and made self-sufficiency my principle from the beginning. I do not need to mention Babylon, and the part of India that lies beyond the Caucasus and beyond the river Hyphasis, all of which I travelled through with my character unaffected: my behaviour here and my indifference to profit are sufficiently attested by this Egyptian. He has ascribed wicked acts and plans to me, but never mentioned how much money I committed these crimes for, or what profit I had in mind. He thinks I am such an idiot as to be a magician and yet to commit, for no profit to myself, the crimes others commit for large profits. This is how I hawk my wares, no doubt: "Roll up, you fools, I do magic not for money but free of charge. Your reward will be the privilege of leaving with the object of your desires fulfilled, and mine will be trials and indictments."

(4) 'However, I do not want to stray into a discussion of folly, so I will ask my accuser what subject I should begin

with. There is no need to ask: it was my clothing that he devoted the beginning of his speech to, and, for that matter, what I eat and do not eat. Defend yourself on this charge, divine Pythagoras, since we are on trial for customs that you began and I follow.

'Earth grows everything for mankind, emperor, and those who are willing to live at peace with the animals need nothing: they can gather with their hands or with the plough, depending on the seasons, what the earth produces to feed her sons. But some as it were disobey the earth and sharpen knives against the animals to gain clothing and food. The Indian Brahmans disapproved of this personally and taught the Naked Philosophers of Egypt to disapprove of it too. From there Pythagoras, who was the first Greek to associate with Egyptians, borrowed the principle. He let the earth keep living creatures, but held that what the earth grows is pure, and so lived off that because it was sufficient to feed body and soul. Clothing made from dead creatures, which most people wear, he considered impure; he dressed in linen and, for the same reason, made his shoes of plaited bark. He derived many advantages from his purity, above all that of perceiving his own soul. He had been born in the time when Troy was fighting on behalf of Helen, and he was the most beautiful of the sons of Panthus and the most beautifully equipped. He died so young as to give Homer a subject for a lament,[8] and passed into several bodies according to the law of Adrasteia, whereby souls migrate. Finally he returned to human form and was born the son of Mnesarchides of Samos, so that he became a wise man who had been a barbarian, an Ionian who had been a Trojan, and a man so immortal that he did not even forget he had been Euphorbus. So I have told you the progenitor of my philosophy and confessed that it is not my

8. Pythagoras's earliest incarnation was supposed to be as Euphorbus (cf. I. 1, above). Homer's lament: *Iliad* XVII. 43ff.

invention, but an heirloom that I have received from others.

'For myself, I do not condemn those who fancy birds like the grouse or those from the Phasis or Paeonia which such men fatten for their own dinners, these people who grant their stomach's every wish. I have never indicted anybody because of their fish for which they pay a higher price than the wealthy once paid for the rarest horses. I have never envied anyone because of his purple or clothing which was from Pamphylia or particularly soft. I myself am indicted, believe it or not, because of asphodel and fruits and pure dishes; (5) not even my clothing is respected, but my accuser tried to filch that from me too, on the ground that it is of a kind prized by magicians. Let us leave aside talk about animate and inanimate things, which give a person a reputation for purity or impurity: in what way is linen better than wool? Wool is shorn from the gentlest of animals, one dear to the gods, who do not think it beneath them to herd sheep; in fact either the gods or the myths once thought a sheep worthy to be made of gold. Linen, on the other hand, is sown by chance, and no myth ever made it into gold. Even so the fact that it is not taken from a living creature made the Indians think it pure, and likewise the Egyptians; and for this reason Pythagoras and I have adopted it for our clothing in our discourses, in our prayers or at our sacrifices. It is a pure covering to sleep under, too; the messages that dreams bring to people who live my kind of life are more reliable.

(6) 'Let me defend next the hair I once had, since a charge has been concocted against me for my greyness. My accuser should be no longer the Egyptian but those blond, carefully groomed boys with their strings of lovers and mistresses whom they chase after. They may consider themselves lucky and enviable for their hair and the perfume that drips from it, but they must consider me the personification of repulsiveness and a lover of abstinence from love. This is what I have to say

to them: "You miserable creatures, do not impugn the institution of the Dorians. The practice of wearing long hair comes from the Spartans, and was observed by them at the time when they were at the peak of military success. Sparta had Leonidas for a king, a man who grew his hair to show his courage and inspire respect in his friends and terror in his enemies.[9] That is why the Spartans grow their hair in his honour no less than in honour of Lycurgus or Iphitus.[10] But a wise man's hair should never be touched by iron, because it is impious to apply iron to the part where all his senses have their source, and from which all his oracles come and his prayers issue forth, as well as the speech which is the interpreter of his wisdom. Empedocles[11] actually tied a ribbon of the purest purple around his hair, and strutted around the public places of Greece, composing hymns in which he said he would be a god when he no longer was a mortal: I kept my hair unkempt and never needed such hymns about it, and yet I am exposed to indictments and law-courts. And yet, as far as Empedocles is concerned, I am not sure whether he was celebrating himself or the felicity of mankind in his day, when such things were not grounds for prosecution."

(7) 'That is enough talk about my hair, because it has been cut off and the charge has been removed by hatred. But because of hatred I have to defend myself against another accusation, a harsh one and of a kind to inspire terror not only in you, emperor, but in Zeus himself. The accuser says that men consider me a god, and avow as much publicly because of the spell I cast on them. But before making that accusation he should have shown what it was that I said, what the amazing

9. Leonidas valiantly led the Spartans at Thermopylae (480 B.C.) until the last man was dead.

10. Lycurgus was the reputed author of the Spartan constitution; Iphitus was the reputed founder of the Olympic games.

11. Empedocles of Acragas (Agrigento in Sicily) was a philosopher and poet of the fifth century B.C.

speech or act was, by which I induced human beings to pray to me. I did not announce before the Greeks what my soul had changed into or changed from in the past, or what it will in future, even though I know; I have never put out such ideas about myself; I never resorted to predictions or to composing oracles as the swarms of diviners do; and I know of no city in which it was ever decided to assemble and sacrifice to Apollonius. And yet I have put them all deeply in my debt, whenever they made requests of me, and their requests were for such things as cures for the sick, greater sanctity in their mysteries or in their sacrifices, the purgation of violence or the strengthening of the laws. My reward for all this was to see them grow in justice, and it was also a benefit to you. Herdsmen who keep their cows in control benefit the owners of the cows; shepherds fatten their sheep to the profit of the owners; beekeepers cure their swarms from disease so that the landlord does not lose his bees; and similarly when I corrected the faults of cities, it was for you that I set them right, and if they had thought me a god, the illusion would have been to your benefit: they would have obeyed me with alacrity because they were afraid to do what a god disapproved of. In fact they did not think this: they only thought that man had some kinship with god, and because of it he is the only creature who is aware of the gods, and speculates about his own nature and the respects in which he shares divinity. Man claims also to be like god in form, as the arts of sculpture and painting make clear, and he believes that the virtues come from god, and that those who share them are close to the gods and godlike. We should not ascribe this belief to the teaching of the Athenians, although they were the first to give such titles as "the Just" and "the Olympian",[12] which are perhaps titles too godlike for men, but rather to the teaching of Apollo at Delphi.

12. Aristides was called 'the Just' (cf. VII. 21, above), Pericles 'the Olympian' (cf. Aristophanes, *Acharnians*, 530).

Lycurgus of Sparta, just after drawing up the laws by which
Sparta is governed, once came to Apollo's shrine: and when
Apollo addresses him in the oracle, he weighs the beliefs about
Lycurgus, saying at the beginning that he is unsure whether to
call him a god or a man, but as he proceeds he assigns and
awards that title to him, as a man of virtue. Yet this never
caused the Spartans to launch any investigation or trial
against Lycurgus on the ground that he claimed immortality,
just because he did not reprove the Pythian god for speaking
to him in this way. In fact they agreed with the shrine, and no
doubt had been already convinced about this matter even
before the oracle. As for the Indians and Egyptians, the
Egyptians criticize the Indians in every way, and speak ill of
their beliefs about material objects: but they have such a high
opinion of the Indians' doctrine about the creator of the universe that they teach it to others, although it is Indian.

'This doctrine recognizes god as the creator of the universe
in its origin and in its essence. What inspired him to this act
was goodness; and since the ideas are related to one another, I
affirm the Indians' doctrine and believe that men who are good
have some share in godhead. The order formed by god's
creation must be understood to be everything in heaven and
sea and earth, in all of which all men have an equal share,
except if chance forbids them. But there is also a kind of order
dependent on a good man, which does not transgress the
bounds set by wisdom; and you yourself, emperor, will not
deny that this needs a man formed in the image of god. What
form, then, does it take? Souls that are undisciplined make a
frenzied attack on every kind of rule; they consider the laws
obsolete, reject all control, and dishonour the honours paid to
the gods; they love gossip and extravagance, which give rise
to a kind of idleness that is wicked and prepared to urge any
course. Souls that are drunken jump from one act to another,
and this frivolity can be checked by nothing, not even if they

were to drink everything devised to induce sleep, like mandragora. What is needed is a man who will ensure order in the souls of others, a god sent to men by wisdom. Such a person has the power to divert souls from passions by which men are carried away in a frenzy deleterious to usual relationships, and to divert them from avarice, which makes men say they do not have enough, just because they are not catching a stream of wealth in their open mouths. As for restraining men's souls from venturing on murder, that is something which is perhaps not impossible for such a man, but to absolve murder is neither in my power nor in that of god, the creator of all.

(8) 'Let me also defend myself, emperor, in the matter of Ephesus and its rescue, and let the Egyptian accuse me as the indictment requires. The accusation runs as follows. "Suppose that there is, in the land of the Scythians or the Celts, who live on the Danube or the Rhine, a city of no less importance than Ephesus in Ionia. This is a base for barbarians who are not your subjects, and it was about to be wiped out by plague when Apollonius cured it.'' Even against this charge a wise man has a defence, if the emperor is the kind of man who is prepared not to use disease, but only war, to extirpate his enemies; I hope that neither you, emperor, nor I ever cause a city to be wiped out, and that I may never see disease in holy places, which will cause them to be filled with sick men. But let us grant that we feel no concern for barbarians, and that we do not count them among sound men, because they are our greatest enemies and irreconcilable with our own race. But who will rob Ephesus of the chance to be cured? It is a city founded at the very origin of the race from the most sacred land of Attica; it has grown greater than all the cities of Ionia and Lydia; it has advanced to the sea, after outgrowing the land on which it was founded; it is a centre for philosophical and rhetorical studies, which make a city strong not in mere horses but in the abundance of its citizens, because it pursues

wisdom. Do you think any wise man would shirk a fight in which such a city was at stake, when he remembered Democritus, who once freed Abdera from plague, or when he thought of Sophocles of Athens, who is said to have calmed the winds when they blew too fierce for summer, or when he had heard of Empedocles's deed, who checked the fury of a rainstorm that burst over Acragas?

(9) 'My accuser is interrupting me, as you too can hear, emperor, and says that the charge against me is not that I caused the Ephesians to be cured but that I foretold to them that the plague would attack them; this, he says, is more than wisdom, it is supernatural, and I would not have attained such a degree of clairvoyance unless I were a magician with secret powers. What would Socrates say to this in defence of the information he claimed to have had from his guardian spirit? Or Thales and Anaxagoras, the Ionians, of whom one predicted a heavy crop of olives and the other predicted many celestial events? Are they to say that they did this through magic? True, they were brought to court on other charges, but nowhere among these charges is it specified that they were magicians because they had foreknowledge. That would have been thought ridiculous, and even in Thessaly would not have been a plausible accusation against men, even though women there had a bad reputation for bringing down the moon.[13]

'How, then, did I discern the disaster at Ephesus? You have heard my accuser say that my diet is different from that of other men, and I too said at the beginning of my speech that my food is light and more pleasant than the luxurious dishes of others. This, emperor, keeps my senses in a kind of mysterious clarity, and prevents cloudiness from affecting them; and

13. Thessaly was famous for its witches and for magic generally. Note, for example, that it is the scene of Goethe's Classical *Walpurgisnacht* in *Faust*.

causes me to discern everything that is and will be, as if it were reflected in a mirror. A wise man will not wait for the earth to give off vapours, or the air to be corrupted, if it is from above that the disaster is to fall. He will perceive these events when they are on the threshold, later than the gods but sooner than other men: the gods are aware of things before they happen, men when they happen, and wise men when they are about to happen. But the causes of disease you should ask me about privately, emperor, because they are too arcane to be described before ordinary people. Now, I ask you, does this kind of diet merely induce a refinement of the senses, or an improvement of them so as to perceive things which are very portentous and amazing?

'You may judge what I mean from many circumstances, but not least from what occurred at Ephesus during that epidemic. The disease took a form like that of an old beggar, and I noticed it, and by doing so overcame it. I did not cure the disease but eradicated it, and the power to which I prayed you may guess from the image which I set up in gratitude: it is that of Hercules the Averter. I took him as my helper because he was clever and brave, and once purged Elis of a plague by washing away the exhalations that rose from the earth when Augeas was tyrant. Do you think that someone who was ambitious to be considered a magician, emperor, would make a dedication to a god out of his own achievement? What admirers for his magical powers would he win if he yielded the claim for admiration to a god? What magician would pray to Hercules? Those scoundrels ascribe such acts to trenches and to the gods of the earth, among whom we must not count Hercules because he is undefiled and a friend of mankind. I also prayed to him once in the Peloponnese, since there was a ghostly vampire staying there too, near Corinth, which loved a handsome young man.[14] Hercules helped me in

14. Above, IV. 10 (Ephesus), 25 (Corinth).

my struggle, and did not ask for any unusual reward, but only for honey-cake, frankincense, and the pleasure of doing something for the preservation of mankind: it was the same thing that he also counted as the fee for his labours in the time of Eurystheus. Do not let it annoy you, emperor, to hear the name of Hercules: Athena took care of him, because he was virtuous and a saviour of mankind.

(10) 'Since you want me to defend myself in the matter of the sacrifice, as you signify by your gesture, hear a true defence. I would do anything to save my fellow men, but I have never made a sacrifice for them, nor would I do so. I would never touch offerings in which there was blood, or pray with my eyes on a knife or on the kind of sacrifice my accuser alleges. I am not a Scythian captive, emperor, or from some uncivilized place; I have never visited the Massagetae or the Tauri, and in fact I would have made them give up their kind of sacrifice. I often discuss the art of prophecy and what its strengths and weaknesses are, and I know better than any man that the gods reveal their intentions to holy and wise men, even if they do not practise divination; and it would be a stroke of folly in me to associate with slaughter, with entrails which I consider unacceptable and unpropitious. If I had, the voice of my guardian spirit would have deserted me as an unclean being. But, leaving aside the pollution entailed by the sacrifice, if you were to interrogate my accuser in the light of what he said a short while ago, he himself acquits me of guilt. According to him, I predicted the plague to the Ephesians without needing to make any sacrifice, and what need did I have of victims in order to learn something I could know without a sacrifice? Why did I need divination in a matter about which I and others were convinced?

'If I am on trial because of Nerva and his friends, I will repeat what I said the other day, when you made this charge. I think Nerva fit for any kind of power, and for all the praise that a good reputation attracts, but I do not think him a good person to contend with responsibilities. His body has been weakened by disease, which has also made his mind full of disgust for the world, so that it is not even up to domestic cares. He admires you for your physique and your intelligence, and is right to do so in my opinion, because human nature is very much more inclined to praise the deeds which it lacks strength to do itself. Nerva also has a kind attitude to me; I have never known him to laugh at me or make any of the usual jokes that friends do, but instead he treats me as a boy treats his father or his own teacher. He invariably minds his language in my presence, and in fact he blushes: and knowing that I praise moderation, he practises it to such an excessive degree that even I think him more retiring than he should be. How could anyone plausibly think that Nerva desired power, when he is satisfied if he can run his own house? Or that he could talk with me on important matters, when he has not had the courage to do so even on trivial ones? Or that he would make such a plan with me, when he would not even make it with anybody else if he respected me? How could I be a wise man, if I trusted to divination in order to foretell the outcome of his plan, and did not trust wisdom? Orfitus and Rufus, however, are just as self-controlled, but unambitious, as I know well, and if anybody says they are suspected for desiring to be tyrants, I do not know whom he is more mistaken about, them or Nerva; but if those two are accused of urging Nerva on, I do not know whether it is harder to believe that Nerva is aiming at power or that they are urging him to.

(11) 'A man who accused me because of these men should have considered something else: what the point was in my conspiring with revolutionaries. He does not allege that I got money from them, or that I was induced by presents to take this course. Let us suppose that I asked for a large fee, but deferred my rewards from them to the time when they

expected to have power, and when I would be in a position to ask for much and to be granted even more. What would be the proofs of this? Consider yourself, emperor, and those who held power before you, your brother and father and Nero, in whose time these men held office; because it has been in these reigns that I have spent most of my public life, whereas previously I was on a visit to India. Now in all those thirty-eight years, since it is that length of time down to the present, I have never paid court to an emperor, except to your father in Egypt, though he was not in fact emperor yet, and made no secret of having come to see me; I have never spoken in a servile manner to emperors or about them before the masses; I have never prided myself on letters sent to me by emperors or written by me to them for public display; never have I deserted my principles by fawning on emperors for gifts. If someone were to consider the two classes of rich and poor and ask me which of them I counted myself as belonging to, I would say the very rich, since my self-sufficiency is in my eyes as good as Lydia and the whole of the river Pactolus. Was I likely, therefore, to postpone gifts from men who were not yet emperors to the time when I thought they would be in power, when I have never accepted gifts from you, even though I thought you secure in your power? Was I likely to plot a change of reigns, when I have never taken advantage of the established one to get honour for myself? Euphrates's position shows all that a philosopher can earn by fawning on the powerful; what he has from that source I cannot call mere money – he has streams of wealth, and nowadays he gives his lectures at the bank, turning himself into a retailer, a petty retailer, a money-collector, a usurer, everything that is sold or engages in sale. He is always glued to the doors of the powerful, and stands at them longer than the porters do, and in fact he has often stayed after the porters have gone, like a ravening dog. While he has never spared a penny for a philosopher, he uses his own riches as a weapon against others, so that he is feeding this Egyptian here on money and sharpening against me this fellow's tongue, which deserves to be cut out. (12) I leave Euphrates to you. Unless you approve of flatterers, you will find the creature worse than I have described.

'Now hear the rest of my defence. If you want to know what it is concerned with, emperor, the accusation contained a dirge sung for an Arcadian boy. They say he was slaughtered by me at night (I don't know if the accuser means it was in a dream), and this boy was supposedly of good pedigree and as handsome as Arcadians can be in their poverty. This boy, they say, was slaughtered despite his entreaties and sobs, and I dipped my hands in his blood and prayed the gods to reveal the truth. Thus far I am the accused: the next part of their speech attacks the gods, because they say that the gods heard me when I made this prayer, and gave me a favourable omen and did not kill me for my impiety.

'I do not need to say that this is pollution even to hear: but as to the part about which I must defend myself, who is this Arcadian? Unless he was of unknown ancestry, or of servile appearance, it is time that you asked what his parents were called, what family he belonged to, what city in Arcadia he grew up in, what altars he was torn away from to be sacrificed here. The accuser doesn't say, although he is clever at not telling the truth. So he must be accusing me because of a slave. If neither the boy nor his parents had a name, if he has no city nor property, must we not class him as a slave, for heaven's sake? Because there are no names anywhere. Then who sold me the slave? Who brought him from Arcadia? If that race is suitable for the kind of divination that uses bloodshed, the boy must surely have been bought for a large sum of money, and somebody must have sailed to the Peloponnese to bring him here for us. Slaves from Pontus or Lydia or Phrygia can be bought in Rome, because you may see droves of them being sent here. Those races, and indeed every barbarian one, are always the subjects of others and so do not consider slavery a disgrace; in fact the Phrygians have the practice of selling their own kin and not caring if they are enslaved. The Greeks, however, are still lovers of freedom, and a Greek will not even sell a slave across his own borders, and that is why no slaver or slave-merchant may visit them. Still less may they visit the Arcadians, because these are not only the most independent of all Greeks, but also need masses of slaves.

'Arcadia is very fertile, and heavily wooded not only on the mountains but everywhere you turn. They need many farmers, goatherds, swineherds, shepherds and herdsmen for their cattle and their horses, and the land needs many wood-cutters, who are trained from boyhood. Even supposing that Arcadia was not like this, and that they were able to sell their extra slaves as other races are: what help was it to my supposed powers of wisdom that the victim was from Arcadia? The Arcadians are not the wisest of the Greeks, so that their innards are in some way more revealing for prophetic purposes than those of other men; in fact they are the most boorish people on earth, and resemble pigs in that they stuff themselves with acorns, as well as in other ways. Perhaps my defence has become rather more rhetorical than is characteristic of me, when I describe the ways of the Arcadians and my discourse takes me to the Peloponnese.

'What kind of defence is appropriate? I did not sacrifice, I do not; I do not touch blood, even if it is on the altar, since that was the doctrine of Pythagoras and that of his followers no less; it was the doctrine of the Naked Philosophers of Egypt and the Wise Men of India, from whom Pythagoras and his sect derived the seeds of their philosophy. Those who sacrifice like that are not considered wicked by the gods: in fact the gods grant them a long life, with their bodies free from impairment and disease; they grant them ever-increasing wisdom, indifference to tyranny, and self-sufficiency. It is not implausible, I think, that such men make virtuous requests when their sacrifices are pure. It is my belief that the gods share my opinion about sacrifices, and therefore have planted the parts of the world that bear incense in an undefiled region of the earth, so that we can use their products to sacrifice without touching iron in holy places or spilling blood on altars. Yet it is claimed that I forgot myself and the gods, and sacrificed in a way that is uncharacteristic of me, and in which I wish no man would sacrifice.

(13) 'The time mentioned by my accuser for the crime may acquit me from blame too. On the day when he says I performed these acts, if I was in the countryside, I sacrificed, and if I sacrificed, I ate. And yet, emperor, you keep asking me whether I was not in Rome at the time. You were too, excellent emperor, but you would not confess to having performed such a sacrifice; so was that informer, but he will not confess he was acting like a murderer, just because he was staying in Rome; and so were thousands of people, whom it would be kinder to expel than to expose to a trial in which it is regarded as a proof of guilt that one was in Rome. Yet, if I had come to Rome, that perhaps frees me from the charge of appearing to plot revolution; because living in a city in which everything is seen and everything is reported, whether true or false, prevents anyone from attempting revolution unless he has suicidal tendencies, and in fact it causes the more cautious and restrained to take even permissible steps only with circumspection.

(14) 'What then was I doing that night, you informer? If I were you and you were asking me, since you take the liberty of asking, I was preparing dangers and accusations against virtuous men, ruin for the innocent, falsehoods of which to convince the emperor so as to bring glory on myself and pollution on him. If you were to ask me as a philosopher, I

was approving of the laughter of Democritus which all human affairs inspire in him. But if you ask me as myself, Philiscus of Melos, who had studied with me for four years, was ill at the time, and I was staying at his house to nurse him: in fact his condition was so bad that he died of the disease. I could have prayed to have many spells to bring him back to life, and to know any melody of Orpheus for restoring the dead; in fact I think I would have gone to the underworld for his sake if it were penetrable. I had become so attached to him because he was a philosopher after my own heart.

'You may hear all this, emperor, from Telesinus the consular, who also attended the man from Melos, looking after him at night just as I did. If you do not believe Telesinus because he is one of those that study philosophy, I call the doctors as witnesses, Seleucus of Cyzicus and Stratocles of Sidon: ask them if what I am saying is true. They were accompanied by more than thirty pupils who no doubt will testify to the same effect; though to summon the relatives of Philiscus you may perhaps think would delay the case, since they left Rome immediately for Melos in order to bury the body. Step up, witnesses, because of course that is why you are here.'

(*The witnesses testify.*)

'How far this fabricated indictment is from the truth these men's evidence clearly shows. I was not in a suburb, but in the city, not outside the wall but in a house, not with Nerva but Philiscus, not committing murder but praying for a man's life, not choosing a new emperor to replace you, but trying to save a man like myself.

(15) 'What is the Arcadian doing in all this, then? Or the nonsense about a victim? Or the attempt to prove this kind of thing? What never happened will happen, if it is judged to have happened.

226

'What will you make of the implausible description of the sacrifice, emperor? In the past there have been men who prophesied from victims, and were clever at their art, and worthy of fame: Megistias of Acarnania, Aristander from Lycia, Silanus who came from Ambracia. The Acarnanian sacrificed for Leonidas king of Sparta, and the Lycian for Alexander of Macedon, and Silanus for Cyrus when he passionately desired the throne. If there was something especially indicative, revealing, or reliable hidden in human entrails, a victim for the sacrifices could have been supplied, since the sponsors were kings, and the kings had many stewards and many captives; they could commit crime with impunity and had no need to fear an accusation if they shed blood. I imagine, however, that those diviners had the same idea as now occurs to me, as I face trial on these charges. Dumb animals, when they are slaughtered without knowing what death is, very possibly do not undergo some obscuration of the entrails, because they do not realize what is about to happen to them; but a man always has in his heart some fear of death even when it is not before him, and when death is at last present before his eyes, how can his entrails possibly give some divinatory sign or any propitious sign at all? You may tell from what follows, emperor, that my guess on this matter is correct and scientific.

'It is the liver that contains the tabernacle of the prophetic art practised by those expert in such matters, so they claim. This is not composed of pure blood, but all the blood that is unpolluted is contained in the heart and channelled by it through the blood-carrying veins throughout the body. The bile lies on the surface of the liver, and is roused by anger, but fear draws it into the recesses of the liver. Now stimulation to anger makes the bile seethe until it can no longer be contained by its own vessel but flows over the edge of the liver, and on these occasions a flood of bile covers the soft and prophetic part of the gut; but stimulation to fear makes it collect, and carry with it all the illumination in the soft parts, since at such times the pure part of the blood also settles, and makes the liver distend by circulating naturally through the tissue that surrounds the liver and by covering the surface of that obscure organ.

'What point, then, emperor, is there in polluted murder if the victim is going to be unresponsive? It is made unresponsive by human nature, which foresees death, and by the behaviour of the dying themselves: the courageous feel anger when they die, and the timid, fear. Hence it is that among those barbarians who have some intelligence, this science favours she-goats and sheep as victims, because these creatures are stupid and practically insensible: but it does not consider suitable for its mysterious practices spirited animals like the cock, boar or bull. I am aware, emperor, that I am annoying my accuser because I have made you a more knowledgeable listener and you seem to me to be attending to my speech: (16) but if there is any part of it that is not clear, I give you permission to question me.

'I have finished answering the Egyptian's indictment. However, I should not, I think, overlook the insinuations of Euphrates, so you must judge, emperor, which of us is the truer philosopher. He is concerned to speak no truth about me, whereas I think that unworthy: he considers you his master, but I consider you my ruler: he gives you a sword to use against me, and I give you reason to use against him.

'The subject of his insinuation is the speeches I made in Ionia, in which he says I spoke against your interests. The Fates and Necessity were my subject, and the illustration which I used for the discourse was taken from the fortunes of kings, because yours seems the highest of all human estates. I talked about the strength of the Fates, and how the threads

they spin are so unalterable that if the goddesses have allotted
a throne to someone when it belongs to someone else, and the
incumbent kills the other so as never to be deprived of his
power by him, the murdered man would come to life again,
because of the decision of the Fates. We employ exaggerated
language because people do not credit the credible: it is as
though I were to say, for instance, that if a man is destined to
be a carpenter and his hands are cut off, he will still be a carpenter; or if he is destined to win in the foot-race at Olympia
and his leg is maimed, he will still not be cheated of his victory;
or if the Fates have allotted him skill at archery and he loses his
eyesight, he will still hit the mark. When I referred to the
fortunes of kings, I meant those like Acrisius, of course, or
Laius, Astyages the Mede and many others, who seemed to
look after their own interests when in power; some of them
thought they had killed their sons, others their grandsons, and
yet they lost their thrones to them, because their victims rose
from obscurity with the help of fate.

'If I were fond of flattery, I would have said I had your own
history in mind, when you were penned in by Vitellius in
Rome, and the temple of Jupiter was set on fire at the summit
of the city,[15] and he thought that all would be well for him if
you did not escape, though you were only a youth, not yet as
old as you now are; even so, the Fates decided otherwise, and
he died despite all his plots, while you now have his place. But
I dislike the music of flattery because it seems to me to be of
the unrhythmical and grating kind, so I will snap this string.
You may consider that I did not have your history in mind at
all, but that my discourse was concerned only with the Fates
and Necessity: whereas it was in that discourse that my accuser
says I was attacking you.

'Yet this doctrine is tolerable even to most of the gods.
Zeus himself is not annoyed when the poets say in their tales of

15. In A.D. 69: cf. Tacitus, *Histories* III. 71.

Lycia, "Alas for me, since Sarpedon ..."[16] and include in their songs the speech in which he says he yields his son to the Fates, or when they say in the "Weighing of Souls" that on the death of Minos, the brother of Sarpedon, he granted him a golden sceptre and appointed him judge in the court of Aidoneus, and did not intercede for him with the Fates.[17] Why does the doctrine annoy you, emperor, when the gods, whose estate is established for ever, find it tolerable, and do not kill the poets for propagating it? It is right that we should obey the Fates and not fight the mutability of fortune, or disbelieve Sophocles when he says:

> 'the gods alone
> are free eternally from age and death:
> all other things all-powerful time destroys,'[18]

words of extraordinary truth. The successes of men go in cycles,[19] and their glory lasts but a day, emperor: what was mine is this man's, what was his is another's, and if this man has that one's goods, he does not really have them. With that in mind, emperor, put an end to exile, an end to bloodshed, treat philosophy as you like, because true philosophy is indifferent, but take away men's tears. At present endless wailing comes from the sea, and much more from the continents, as all of them mourn what makes them mourn. The evils that have their root in Rome are too many to be counted, and they are due to the tongues of informers who slander all to you and you, emperor, to all.'

16. *Iliad* XVI. 433.

17. *Odyssey* XI. 568.

18. *Oedipus at Colonus*, 607.

19. For similar ancient views of the instability of human fortunes, cf. Herodotus I. 5. 4; Thucydides I. 22 and III. 82. 2; Tacitus, *Annals* III. 55. The concept of cycles is not deterministic; it implied constant shifting: see Ludwig Edelstein, *The Idea of Progress in Classical Antiquity*, 1967.

8. This is how Apollonius's prepared speech ran. At the end of it I found the end of his other speech, 'You will not slay me, since I am not mortal',[20] and the earlier part of the speech from which this line comes as well.

Apollonius left the court by some supernatural, inexplicable means. The emperor did not react in the way he was generally expected to. Everyone thought he would roar with indignation, start a hunt for Apollonius, and make an announcement through all of his empire that no one was to admit the philosopher. He did none of this, as if he were deliberately controverting the general opinion, or had realized at last that he had no power against Apollonius. Whether he thought Apollonius beneath his notice may be judged from the sequel, in which it may be seen that he felt confusion rather than contempt.

9. He began to listen to another case after that one, which involved a city disputing a will with an individual, I think. The emperor forgot not only the names of the parties but even the point of the dispute, because his questions were pointless and his answers were not even relevant to the hearing. This clearly proved that the tyrant was dazed and lost, for the very reason that he had been convinced by his flatterers that he could not forget anything.

10. This was the state Apollonius put the tyrant into, and proved that to someone of his own wisdom the man before whom all Greeks and barbarians trembled was child's play. Apollonius left the court before noon, and about evening was seen by Demetrius and Damis in Dicaearchia. This was the reason why he had urged Damis not to wait for his defence, but to go by land to Dicaearchia: he did not reveal his plans, but told his closest friend to do something that proved to be in accordance with them.

20. cf. VIII. 4, above.

11. Damis had arrived the day before, and had conversed with Demetrius about the events leading up to the hearing. The information put Demetrius into a more timid frame of mind than was to be expected when Apollonius was the subject, and the next day he began to question Damis on the same issue, loitering with him beside the sea: it is here that the tales about Calypso are set.[21] They had despaired of his ever coming back since there was a universal dread of the tyrant's power, but still they obeyed Apollonius's orders because of his endowments. In dejection, they had gone to sit in the grotto of the Nymphs in which the jar stands: this is a jar of white stone containing a spring of water, which neither flows over the edge nor goes down if it is drawn from. They were discussing the explanation of the water, without very much interest because of their despondency over Apollonius, and were returning to the subject of the events preceding the hearing.

12. Damis groaned out loud, and said something like, 'Gods above, will we ever see our good, noble comrade?'

Apollonius, who was now standing at the entrance to the grotto, heard this and said, 'You will, in fact you already have.'

'Alive?' asked Demetrius. 'But if dead, we have never stopped weeping for you.'

Apollonius stretched out his hand, and said, 'Take hold of me. If I elude you, I am a ghost come back from Persephone's domain, like the ghosts which the gods below reveal to men when mourning makes them too despondent. But if I stay when you grasp me, persuade Damis too that I am alive and have not lost my body.'[22]

21. cf. *Odyssey* V.

22. cf. Christ before the Apostles after his resurrection: Luke XXIV. 39, 'Behold my hands and my feet, that it is I myself: handle me and see.' Similarly, John XX. 20, 27.

Unable to disbelieve any longer, they stood up, hugged Apollonius, welcomed him, and asked him about his defence. Demetrius thought that he had not even made one, because he would have been put to death despite his innocence, while Damis thought he had made one, but perhaps rather earlier, not that very day.

'I have made my defence,' said Apollonius, 'and I have won my case. The defence took place today, not long ago: it was getting on for midday.'

'How have you come such a distance in so small a part of the day?' asked Demetrius.

'You may imagine what you like, except that I used a ram or wings made of feathers.[23] Consider a god responsible for my return.'

'I always think that some god watches over your actions and words everywhere,' said Demetrius, 'and is the cause of your present fortune. But tell us all about your defence, how it went, what the charges were, how your judge behaved, what he asked, where he agreed with you and where he didn't. Then I can tell the details to Telesinus, who will never stop asking how you fared. A fortnight or so ago, when he was dining with me in Antium, he fell asleep at the table, half way through his drink. He dreamed that the earth was flooded by fire, which engulfed some, overtook others as they fled before it, since it ran as fast as water, but did not affect you as it did the rest: it parted for you to pass through. After this dream he made a libation to the gods that give good advice, and encouraged me to be cheerful about you.'

'I am not surprised that Telesinus overslept,' said Apollonius; 'long ago he kept awake over me. I will tell you about the trial, though not here, since it is now well into the evening and time to go into the town. Conversation along the way

23. Allusions to the ram (of the golden fleece) by which Nephele tried to save her children, and to the wings of Icarus.

would be a pleasant companion for our walk. Let us go, then, exchanging talk on whatever you ask me about, and I will tell you what happened in court today. You both know what led up to the trial, you because you were there, Damis, and you, Demetrius, because you have presumably heard about it, goodness knows, not once but many times, unless I have forgotten my Demetrius. I will recount what you do not yet know, beginning from the notification and my entering stripped naked.' So he recounted his own remarks, closing with 'You shall not slay me', and the way he left the court.

13. At that point Demetrius shouted, 'I thought you were safe when you arrived: but this is only the beginning of your dangers. He will outlaw you and have you denied all refuge until he arrests you.'

Apollonius ignored Demetrius's fears. 'I wish he could catch you as easily! But I know how matters stand with him at present. After having always listened to words of flattery, he has now listened to words of rebuke; and these make tyrants lose their temper and fly into a fury. But I have still not rested my limbs after the fight, and I need rest.'

'Demetrius,' said Damis, 'my feelings about Apollonius's situation were such that I tried to dissuade him from the journey he has now come back from. You gave him the same advice, that he should not walk into grave dangers of his own free will. But at the time when he was in bonds, or so I thought, and I considered his position hopeless, he said it was in his power to be rescued; and he showed me his leg freed from its chain. That was the first time I understood him, and realized that he was godlike and above the wisdom of us humans. So, even if I were to fall into a graver predicament, I would never be afraid with his protection, even in danger. But evening is near, so let us go to our lodging to attend to Apollonius.'

'I need nothing but sleep,' he said, 'everything else is all the same to me, whether I have it or whether I don't.' Then he prayed to Apollo and to the Sun too, and entered the house in which Demetrius was living. There he had his feet washed, and urged Damis and the others to have dinner, because they looked hungry: and so he threw himself down on his bed and went to sleep, after first singing the line of Homer in praise of it,[24] as if the present circumstances were not worth worrying about.

14. At about daybreak Demetrius asked him where on earth he was going to travel to. He himself imagined he could already hear the thud of horsemen whom he thought would come at any moment for Apollonius, sent by the furious tyrant.

'Neither he,' said Apollonius, 'nor anyone else will pursue me. My course, however, is for Greece.'

'A dangerous one,' said Demetrius, 'since it is a very difficult country to hide in. You could not escape him in concealment, and how will you elude him in the open?'

'I do not need to,' replied Apollonius; 'if the whole earth belongs to the tyrant, as you imagine, it is better to die in the open than to live in concealment.' Then addressing Damis he said, 'Do you know of a ship sailing for Sicily?'

'Yes,' he replied; 'we are staying near the sea, the crier is near the door, and the ship is getting ready now, as I can tell from the shouting of the crew and their concern with weighing anchor.'

'Let us take this ship, Damis,' said Apollonius, 'and sail to Sicily for the present, and thereafter to Greece.'

'I agree,' said Damis. 'Let us sail.'

15. They said good-bye to Demetrius, who was worried about them, and told him to be cheerful for them and be a man as

24. *Iliad* XIV. 233.

they were. Then they sailed for Sicily with a favouring wind, and by way of Messina reached Tauromenium in three days. Next they put in at Syracuse, and then set off for the Peloponnese about the beginning of autumn. After crossing the open sea, they arrived after five days at the mouth of the Alpheus, at the point where the river enters the Adriatic and Sicilian seas, still fresh. They disembarked, and, delighted to have reached Olympia, stayed in the sanctuary of Zeus, never going away further than Scillus. The Greek world buzzed everywhere with the news that Apollonius was alive and had come to Olympia. At first the rumour was thought to be unfounded. Apart from the fact that they had no earthly hope for him once they had heard he was in prison, they had also heard other stories: Apollonius had been burnt to death, he had been dragged still living with hooks fastened in his collarbones, he had been thrown down a crevasse or into the deep. But when they were sure he had come, the Greeks flocked together in their excitement to see him, as they never had for the Olympics. The Eleans and the Spartans came from near by, the Corinthians from the borders of the Isthmus, while the Athenians, even though they are outside the Peloponnese, were as numerous as those from the cities at the very outskirts of Pisa;[25] the most distinguished of the Athenians came to the sanctuary, as well as the youths that come to Athens from all parts of the world. Some visited Olympia from Megara on that occasion, as did many from Boeotia, Argos, and all the prominent men from Phocis and Thessaly. Some had previously sat at Apollonius's feet, and wished to acquire new wisdom, expecting that they would receive more lessons of even greater marvel; others did not know him, but were ashamed to be thought not to have heard so great a man. When he was asked how on earth he had escaped the tyrant, he was never led to boast, but said he had made his defence and

25. A city in the Peloponnese.

got off. But many visitors from Italy gave the news of what had happened in court, until Greece could barely keep from doing obeisance to him; he was inspired, they thought, precisely because he never resorted to boasting about his past.

. . . . .

19. After he had held discussions in Olympia for forty days, and covered many subjects, he said, 'Men of Greece, I will converse with you in your several cities, at your festivals, your processions, your mysteries, your sacrifices and your libations, because these all require an experienced man. But for the present I must go down to Lebadea since I have never met Trophonius, though I once visited the sanctuary.' With these words he started out for Boeotia, accompanied by all his admirers.

The cave at Lebadea is dedicated to Trophonius the son of Apollo, and may only be entered by those who come for an oracle.[26] The cave may be seen not in the sanctuary but a little way above it on a hill, and is enclosed by a palisade of iron stakes; and the entrance is so sharply inclined as to make even a man sitting down unable to hold back. Visitors dress in white clothing and proceed with honey-cakes in their hands to pacify the serpents that attack those going down to the oracle; and they come up, some near by, some very far away, as when they are carried to beyond Locris and Phocis, but most do so about the borders of Boeotia.

Apollonius entered the sanctuary and said, 'I want to go down with a question about philosophy.' The priests, in order to prevent him, told the multitude that they would never let any magician test the oracle, and to Apollonius they pretended that that particular day was an ill-omened one and not propitious for consulting the oracle. So for that day he held a

26. cf. Pausanias's account of this cave and its oracle: IX. 39. 4–5 (5–14).

discussion at the source of the Hercyna on the origin of the
sanctuary and its method, since it is the only one to give its
responses through the medium of those seeking them. When
evening came, he proceeded to the mouth of the cave with the
younger of his followers, lifted out four of the stakes forming
the entrance door, and advanced below the earth with only
his cloak, just as if he had dressed for a discussion. His behaviour
was so pleasing to Trophonius that the god appeared to his
priests, rebuked them for their treatment of Apollonius, and
told them all to go to Aulis, where Apollonius was to emerge
in the most extraordinary way. Apollonius appeared there
after seven days, the longest period ever spent by any who had
visited the oracle, and he was carrying a book very appropriate to his inquiry. His question when he went down had
been, 'Which of the philosophies, Trophonius, do you consider the most perfect and pure?', and the book contained the
doctrines of Pythagoras, which showed that the oracle too
agreed with this school of philosophy.

20. This book is dedicated at Antium, and is highly regarded
because of the story behind it. Antium is a coastal town of
Italy.[27] The other particulars you may ascertain from the
inhabitants of Lebadea, but I must finish my account of the
book. It was later brought to the emperor Hadrian, at the same
time as certain, though not all, of Apollonius's letters; and it
remained in the palace at Antium, which was his favourite
among the palaces in Italy.

21. There also gathered around Apollonius all his followers
from Ionia, named 'Apollonians' by the Greeks, and they
combined with those in Greece to form a young band,
amazing for its numbers and its eagerness for philosophy.

27. The present translator and editor consider this sentence a gloss,
interpolated into the text.

Public speaking was left in neglect and little attention was paid to manipulators of that art, since it taught only the tongue; everyone flocked to the philosophy of Apollonius. He acted in the way reported of a Gyges or a Croesus, who kept the doors of their treasuries unlocked to let those who needed take their fill: he gave away his wisdom to whoever desired it, and let them ask questions on any subject.

22. He was criticized for avoiding the visits of the governors and preferring to lead his listeners away to quiet places; and when someone joked that he led his sheep to new pastures when he heard advocates coming, he replied, 'Indeed I do, to stop the wolves breaking into the fold.' The meaning of this was as follows. He saw advocates winning general admiration, advancing from poverty to wealth, and welcoming feuds so as to make a trade out of them; he therefore diverted the young from associating with them, and anybody who had already done so he reprimanded with particular sharpness, as if he were washing some ugly dye out of them. He had disapproved of such men even before, but the prisons, with those chained and dying in them, had so disgusted him with the profession that he considered all those disasters more the work of the informers and those who owed their rise to trickery than of the tyrant.

23. About the time when he was lecturing in Greece, there appeared in the sky the following portent. A halo[28] like a rainbow encircled the sun's disc and dimmed its splendour. It was clear to all that the portent signified a revolution, and the governor of Greece summoned Apollonius from Athens to Boeotia and said, 'I hear that you are wise in supernatural matters, Apollonius.'

28. The Greek word here is *stephanos*, meaning wreath or crown: it portends Domitian's murder at the hand of the freedman Stephanus.

'I am, if you also hear that I am so in human matters.'

'I do,' he replied, 'and I believe it.'

'Well, if you assent to that,' said Apollonius, 'do not meddle in the decisions of heaven: that is a rule which human wisdom has approved.'

The man begged Apollonius to say what his interpretation was, because he was afraid that universal night would fall, to which Apollonius said, 'Don't worry: this night will be followed by dawn.'

24. After this, when Apollonius had stayed in Greece for two years and had had enough of it, he sailed to Ionia followed by his disciples. Most of the time he spent holding discussions in Smyrna and Ephesus, though he also went around the other cities. So far from being unwelcome, there was no city in which the cultivated did not miss him after his departure and consider themselves greatly in his debt.

25. The time had come in which the gods were deposing Domitian from his supremacy over mankind. He had just executed Clemens, a man of consular rank, to whom he had given his sister's hand, and had issued an order about two or three days after the murder that she was to join her husband.[29] So Stephanus, a freedman of hers, who was foretold by the shape of the portent,[30] was led by consideration for the murdered man, or for all Domitian's victims, to make a plot against the tyrant equal to that of the most freedom-loving of the Athenians. He tied a knife under his left forearm, and nursed

29. Flavius Clemens, a son of Vespasian's brother, was consul in A.D. 95; he was married to Flavia Domitilla. Their deaths seem to have occurred soon after Clemens's consulate. The charge against them was impiety, and scholars have found reason to believe that they might have been Christians.

30. On the portent and its prophetic shape, see Chapter 23 above, with the note.

his arm in a sling as if he had broken it. Then he approached
Domitian as he was leaving his court and said, 'I must speak
to you alone, emperor; I have an important matter to tell
you.' The tyrant decided not to neglect hearing him, and took
him off to the men's quarters, where the royal chambers were.
'Your chief enemy, Clemens,' said Stephanus, 'is not dead, as
you imagine, but I know where he is, and he is plotting
against you.' The emperor roared out at this news, and
Stephanus, attacking him when he was off his balance, drew
the knife from the concealment of his arm and drove it
through Domitian's thigh; the blow was not so accurate as to
be immediately fatal, but accurate enough to be fatal later.
The emperor, who had always been of strong physique, and
was then about forty-four, grappled with Stephanus after the
blow, knocked him down, and pinned him, and then gouged
his eyes and beat his face with the stem of a golden cup which
had been lying there for use in ritual; at the same time he called
on Athena for help. The bodyguards, realizing he was in
distress, all burst in and killed the tyrant when he was already
sinking.

26. All this happened in Rome, but was seen by Apollonius in
Ephesus. He was holding a discussion in the woods of the park
about noon, the very time when the events in the palace took
place. First he dropped his voice, as if afraid; then his exposi-
tion lost some of its usual clarity, as happens when a man is
distracted by something in the middle of his argument; then
he fell silent, as people do when they have lost the thread. He
stared hard at the ground, stepped three or four paces forward,
and shouted, 'Strike the tyrant! Strike him!' It was not as if
he was observing some reflection of truth through a mirror,
but as if he was seeing the real thing and seeming to take part
in the action.

The Ephesians were all present at the discussion, and were

astounded, until Apollonius, after waiting as people do to see
the result of an even struggle, said, 'Don't worry, my friends.
The tyrant was slaughtered today. Why do I say today? Just
now, I tell you, just now, about the moment when I fell silent
in my talk.' Those in Ephesus thought this was madness, and
although they wanted him to be right, were afraid of the risks
if they listened. 'I am not surprised,' said Apollonius, 'that you
do not believe what I say yet, when not even all of Rome
knows about it. But look, Rome is finding out now; the
rumour is spreading; now ten thousand believe it, now
twice as many are leaping in joy, now twice as many as that,
now four times as many, now all the cities there. This message
will get here too; and you may postpone celebrating with a
sacrifice to the time when the news arrives, but I am going to
thank the gods for what I have seen.'

27. The story had still not gained credence when messengers
came with the good tidings and confirmed Apollonius's
wisdom. The assassination of the tyrant, the day on which it
had come,[31] the noon hour, the assassins whom Apollonius had
urged on, proved to correspond in every detail with what the
gods had revealed to him during his discourse.

Thirty days later a letter came from Nerva that he now held
power in Rome, thanks to the advice of the gods and of Apollonius, but he would retain it more easily if Apollonius came
to advise him.

For the moment, Apollonius wrote back the following
riddle, 'We will be together, emperor, a very long time,
when we have power over no one, and no one over us.'
Perhaps he realized that he himself was to depart from mankind in a very short time, and that Nerva was to rule only
briefly: his reign lasted for a year and four months, and was of
the greatest moderation.

31. 18 September A.D. 96.

28. He did not, however, want to appear to slight a good friend and a good ruler, and so he later composed a letter to him with advice about ruling. Then, calling Damis, he said, 'You are needed for this mission. The contents are secret, and written for the emperor's benefit, and either I must address them to him directly or you must convey them.'

Damis says he only later realized Apollonius's trick, for although he had composed the letter very well and on an important subject, it could safely have been carried by someone else. The point of the trick was this. For all of his life he is said to have observed many times, 'Live unnoticed, but if you cannot, die unnoticed.'[32] So, intending to make Damis leave him and ensure that there were no witnesses when he departed, he used the excuse of the letter and Damis's mission to Rome. Damis says that he was rather moved as he left him, even though he had no idea of what was to happen: but Apollonius, who had a very good one, did not talk to him the way people do when they are never to see each other again, so abundantly was he convinced that he would always exist; and he gave his injunction to Damis, 'Even when you are speculating by yourself, Damis, watch me.'

29. The account of Apollonius of Tyana given by Damis the Assyrian ends with this remark. There are several versions of his death, if he did die, but none is given by Damis. However, this is an item I must not leave out if my story is to have its proper conclusion. Nor has Damis said anything about his friend's age, though some say it was eighty, some that it was over ninety, and some that he easily passed a hundred, in the perfect use and enjoyment of all his body, and with more charm than he had had in youth. There is a certain beauty in wrinkles, and it appeared particularly in Apollonius, as is

32. An adaptation of the Epicurean maxim, 'Live unnoticed' (*lathe biosas*).

shown by the statues of him in the sanctuary at Tyana and by the descriptions which are more lyrical about him as an old man than the accounts used to be of Alcibiades as a young one.

30. Some say he died in Ephesus in the care of two maid-servants (since the freedmen whom I mentioned at the beginning were now dead). When he freed one of these, he was blamed by the other for not showing equal consideration to her, to which he said, 'It is in your interest to be her slave, since that will bring you good fortune.' So when he died the one became the other's slave, until her mistress for some petty reason sold her to a slave-trader. Despite her lack of beauty, a man bought her and fell in love with her; and being a wealthy businessman made her his wife and acknowledged his children by her.

Others say that he died in Lindos after passing into the temple of Athena and vanishing inside. Others recount that he died in Crete, in a way still more extraordinary than is related at Lindos. Apollonius was staying in Crete and receiving even greater admiration than before, when he visited the sanctuary of Dictynna[33] late at night. This shrine is guarded by dogs that protect the treasure in it, and the Cretans consider them no less dangerous than bears or other equally wild animals. But they did not even bark when Apollonius arrived, and instead came up and greeted him, even more than they greeted those they knew best. The officials of the sanctuary arrested Apollonius as a magician and a robber, on the ground that he had thrown something to the dogs to pacify them. But at about midnight he set himself free, and after calling his captors in order to gain their attention, he ran to the doors of the shrine. They flew open, and then, when he had entered, closed to their original position. From inside came the voice of maidens singing, and their song went, 'Proceed from earth!

33. Artemis.

Proceed to heaven! Proceed!' In other words, 'go up from the earth'.[34]

31. He continued to give instruction on the immortality of the soul, and taught that the doctrine about it is true, but discouraged meddling in such important matters. A young man arrived in Tyana who was quick to argue and did not accept the truth. Apollonius had then departed from mankind, but his transformation caused amazement and nobody ventured to deny that he was immortal. Most of the youth's conversations were about the soul, since there was a group of young men there devoted to wisdom, and in the course of denying completely the immortality of the soul, he said, 'My friends here, for nine months now I have never stopped praying to Apollonius to reveal the truth about the soul. But he is so thoroughly dead that he has not even appeared in answer to my request, or persuaded me that he is immortal.' The boy said no more on that occasion: but four days later, he was discussing the same subject when he fell asleep where he had been talking, while the young men with him attended to their books or occupied themselves with drawing geometrical figures on the ground. The boy jumped up from his sleep like a madman, sweating profusely, and shouted, 'I believe you.' The others asked what had happened to him, and he said, 'Don't you see the wise Apollonius as he stands among us listening to our conversation, and gives his marvellous declamation on the soul?'

'Where is he?' they asked. 'We can't see him anywhere, though we would give the world to do so.'

The boy said, 'He must have come to talk to me about what I disbelieved: so let me tell you how he has immortalized the doctrine:

34. The present translator and editor consider 'In other words . . . earth' a gloss, interpolated into the text.

'The soul's an immortal thing, not yours to own
But Providence's. When the body wastes,
Like a swift horse that breaks its bonds, the soul
Leaps nimbly out, and mingles with light air,
Shunning its hated, dreary servitude.
But what is this to you, who when you've gone
Will know it well? And why among the living
Bother yourself with thinking on such things?'

This is the clear testament of Apollonius on the mysteries of the soul, to help us advance with courage and with knowledge of our own natures to the place the Fates assign us. I never yet remember having come across a tomb or cenotaph of Apollonius, although I have travelled over most of the known world, but I have met supernatural stories about him everywhere. There is also a shrine to him at Tyana, built at imperial expense,[35] since emperors have seen fit to grant him the honours granted to themselves.

35. For Caracalla's dedication of a shrine to Apollonius at Tyana, cf. Cassius Dio LXXVII. 18. 4.

INDEX

INDEX